DEDICATION

To the love of my life Cindy

for her lifelong support through thick and thin and for keeping the faith.

Also to my children, grandchildren, family and friends,

thanks for the support.

Also to my colleagues and teams over the years

who have made work fun, rendered the unbearable bearable

and assisted in the accomplishment of some "magic moments."

CONTENTS

Introduction viii

1. Desperate Times Lead to Desperate Measures 1
2. Guess My Secret 13
3. Manifest Destiny - Solving the Puzzle 25
4. Why Did Hogan Not Reveal His Secret? 35
5. Practice, Practice, Practice; Trials and Tribulations
   Lead to a Precipice 41
6. Another Smack at the Wall 51
7. Digging it Out of the Dirt 59
8. Implications 75
9. Now That We Know… 81
10. Getting the Feel of "It" Exemplars.
    Are You a Technolosos or a Feeliosos? 93
11. Why Me? Digging it Out of the Dirt, Too 105
12. Trials and Tribulations, Too 111
13. What Do You Do Once You Know? 129

Bibliography and Resources 137
About the Author 141

INTRODUCTION

"He's the only player I have ever known to get an ovation from the fans on the practice tee. I've seen him playing practice rounds before a tournament and half the gallery was made up of other professionals. Somebody asked me once, who's better? Jack Nicklaus or Ben Hogan? Well, my answer was, I saw Nicklaus watch Hogan practice. But I never saw Hogan watch Nicklaus."
Thomas Henry "Terrible Tommy" Bolt

The very notion that there is a Ben Hogan secret yet to be revealed after all these years remains problematic at best for those who know the story. For someone like me, an occasional golfer not involved in the golf business in any way, to go on record with the premise that I have somehow discovered the secret behind the mystery that has lingered some sixty or more years sounds pretty fanciful, particularly to those around me who I suspect do not understand all the "fuss." But solve it I believe I have!

Ben Hogan's secret, with the passage of time, has taken on the folklore status of the Yeti, Sasquatch or Big Foot, a mystery item like the Bermuda Triangle combined with the mystery of the pyramids and the identity of Shakespeare. The long-rumored potential Holy Grail of golf techniques! The very knowledge of the information is sufficient to transform a dub or terrible golfer into a professional; such is the hype behind the mystique! As with most things in life, the truth will be rather pedestrian in comparison to the folklore surrounding it.

For the past eighteen years I pursued a methodology to improve my golf swing that in hindsight duplicated the trials and tribulations that led Hogan to his breakthrough. I did it on a sporadic basis, but in a consistent manner that initially focused on perfecting the fundamentals of the golf swing but increasingly focused on mastering the fundamentals outlined in Hogan's *Five Lessons: The Modern Fundamentals of Golf*. I was not trying to solve any secret or secrets; my goal was to verify Hogan's premise that a reasonably talented, athletic golfer could consistently break 80, play good golf, and hit good shots by implementing his methodology.

I thank you for taking the time to read this book about Ben Hogan's secret, and partaking in this little "adventure." I call it an adventure because, after you read my premise and the main storyline (assuming you are a golfer), you will no doubt find yourself on the range attempting to verify the assertion outlined herein. It's almost mandatory to do so; you owe it to "us golfers" to kick the tires on this one.

There is no better way to put the issue to bed once and for all than to verify it yourself through a trip to the practice tee or the Hogan golf "laboratory," replete with perspiration, calluses, fundamentals, cobwebs, mystery, discarded tips, tricks, devices, hopes, doubts and fears. And, yes, his secrets. Even if you feel no compunction whatsoever to do so and you can blissfully ignore the insistence of "the man in the glass," much like the elephant you can't keep from your thoughts, you will put it to the test eventually. It is human nature! And when you do, I hope that you approach it with a modicum of seriousness – as seriously as befits the memory of a man so driven to be the best at his chosen field that he dedicated his life and everything he had to the game.

Ben Hogan and others like him who toiled away for so many years in the post-depression and postwar period left much to those who followed in their footsteps. We golfers in general benefited greatly across a number of fronts. But the main beneficiaries are those plying their craft, enjoying what became the modern-day pro-golf tour. I wouldn't expect anyone to approach golf in as serious a manner as he did, obviously, as these were life-and-death struggles for Hogan. In his case we are talking about a man battling himself to achieve his dreams.

So, no, do not approach your rendezvous with destiny or your attempt at validation from *that* serious a viewpoint. Rather approach the matter with the foreknowledge of the single-minded focus and dedication required to achieve the full effect, the fruits of the labor. A better approach is from the appreciative standpoint one might bring to art or landscape design or, as I read the other day, an optimistic golf view that brings you back the next time, regardless of how poorly you play. Any image that conjures up the use of your appreciative eye, rather than your caustic or cynical side, will do. Now I have not said your "agreeable eye" and I do not expect that anyone will bring a "blind eye," or agree to the premises herein without considerable scrutiny. This is a serious matter and I don't expect a free pass. At stake with your trial are the dreams, hopes, and desires of generations of golfer wannabes, perhaps even yourself, one tip away from top-flight golf! So it is probably best to bring your golfing eye, that optimistic, "I'm going to play better today and it's beautiful out here" eye; you always know how it went by the end of the day (and yet you come back, anyway!).

But should you venture to the range using the kind of "serious" approach I described, you will quickly convince yourself either that I missed the boat somehow (because you still don't get "it") or conclude that I just don't know what I am talking about, or that perhaps this exercise is much easier than I make it out to be. However, I believe you will have your own "aha moment" when you successfully execute a few shots for yourself. If that is the case, I suspect that you will join me in renewed enjoyment at the absurdity engendered in the preposterous tail chase we have been treated to these past sixty years or so with regard to the issue of Hogan's "secret."

In the Army we often referred to the "Bottom Line Up Front" (BLUF). While I am perilously close to a mockery of that phrase, the BLUF is that I wrote this book to share my own "aha moment." I experienced it like a lightning strike while working on my golf swing, integrating my interpretation of Ben Hogan's teaching methodology outlined in his *Five Lessons*. Very simply, my effort to master my interpretation of those fundamentals led me to discover the secret of Henny Bogan. The main part of the secret is that Henny Bogan was Ben Hogan! That blinding flash of the obvious (BFO) is much like the knowledge imparted in his book, one of the best-selling golf books of all time, wherein he said, "Good golf begins with a good grip."

Hogan said that more than fifty years ago, but that knowledge is not such a BFO if you visit any local driving range and simply look down the line of golfers. When you take note of the grips in use on the range, you will no doubt see a veritable mixture of grips that belong in the House of Golf Horrors, or with Harley Davidson riders or Dr. Strange Glove candidates. Many golf books make similar observations. Johnny Miller notes in his book, *Pure Golf,* that if you were to walk down the line and observe one hundred golfers at his local driving range, you would likely see one good swing and six or so okay or average swings. The remaining swings are lousy, and the main culprit is likely a faulty grip or just plain bad fundamentals. The experience of observing the local driving range is akin to that which greets the instructors at the cartoon "Acme" bicycle-riding school on the first day, when they haven't yet taught the proper way to face on the bicycle.

If the grip is not a BFO in golf, and it is evident from our range inventory that it is not, then it is clear that much like in life, so it is in golf. That is, nothing is obvious to the uninformed. The average golf book on my shelf contains almost ten pages alone on the grip. Hogan himself in *Five Lessons* discusses the proper grip for about eighteen pages, plus the review, which represents about fifteen percent of his book. Is it possible that almost ninety-three percent of these golfers wandered onto the range that day for the first time? Or do these golfers not read golf books? Or do they not believe what they read in the golf books? Or is there some other rational explanation for this level of, well, ineptitude? In all likelihood there are probably dozens of reasons why these observations remain true.

The main point I am stressing here is that, much like the BFO regarding the grip, knowing what we suspected all along was true (Henny was Hogan) is a good start. To explain the significance of this seemingly simple assertion, I will provide an anti-BFO, so that you can more readily accept the premise and the implications of this argument. Obviously, you can make use of the information and employ it as you see fit, but as an old wing commander used to say (much like the millions of golf readers over the years who have proven immune to that BFO regarding the grip), "If you relearn a lesson, you never learned anything in the first place!"

Now, who is this Henny Bogan character and where does he fit in with all this secretive, "mystiquey" Hogan stuff? Assuming we are all golfers, we've no doubt read with interest some of the books regarding Ben Hogan and his famous secret. These writings have done nothing if not renew my faith in the book classification system! This book is not fiction, fanciful fiction, or "pretend-real"

Introduction

fictional biography. It is not based on something revealed to me personally, or any other fanciful tangential link or lineage offered by way of a name drop to increase my credibility. This book is based on my work, digging information out of the dirt, reading and analyzing the available facts, and applying deductive reasoning – and from hitting golf balls over the last eighteen years or so.

The digging in the practice-range dirt and data-mining of the informational "dirt" involved a lot of enjoyable work! I spent the bulk of this time trying to dig my own swing out until I frankly exhausted just about all the wrong options. I happen to play golf right-handed, hockey left-handed. I even tried to hit some left-handed shots just for grins. But in the final analysis, I simply exhausted all the explorative space and stumbled onto the correct technique somewhere south of ridiculous and north of sublime.

The proof of my discovery can be verified by visiting the range and trying it for yourself. You will know soon enough if it hits the mark, much like the tumblers lining up on a safe combination. But that will only work for the golfer who happens to be one of the decent swingers referenced above who have gone about their golf business in a manner based on solid fundamentals such as those outlined in *Five Lessons*. Attempts to implement the concepts without solid fundamentals would be, to repeat Hogan's admonition from 1955, "ruinous."

Those closely associated with Hogan might be able to verify my premise, although it would probably have to be a true Hogan confidant such as golf analyst Ken Venturi. I suspect that no one else knows the truth about the "secret" or the important role that Henny Bogan played in the discovery. I am convinced Venturi made a vow not to tell. He has consistently just given us basic information and publicly avoided expansion of the answer, such as when he told us the Hogan secret was psychological or "in his head."

I welcome feedback and I stress that my statements within are not offered to challenge other secrets that have been revealed over the years and attributed to Hogan. Those secrets are just as valid today as they were when they were given to those golfers digging their own swings out of the dirt. Hogan blessed them with information in an earnest desire to help them with their swings; but we shouldn't confuse those personal modifications or swing fundamental points of emphasis with Hogan's compensations for his own swing tendencies. We need to separate out the facts and acknowledge those items that are clearly part of his fundamentals included in *Five Lessons,* or in any number of his well-known setup keys. Those are the veritable foundation of the Hogan house per se, his "edge," like the extra cleat on his golf shoe. These items comprise what Jim McLean refers to as "all of it" or the complete body of knowledge that McLean assessed as constituting Hogan's "secret." But these peripheral aspects have little or nothing to do with Hogan's secret for *his* swing, or more appropriately, the methodology by which he resolved his swing issues.

Or, perhaps they have everything to do with it, in the way that ingredients relate to a recipe. Much like a recipe, simply dumping known ingredients in a pan can be disastrous. In point of fact, a good way to wreck the golf swing is by attempting to roll all the known "secrets" into an integrated package as if they were options on an automobile that simply need to be added and connected. Much like the automobile, certain parts go with certain cars and would be out of place on others.

Attempts to swing by emphasizing constituent elements will likely prove similarly disastrous. Imagine trying to hit a golf shot while thinking about rolling the clubface clockwise on the backswing, staying on the proper swing plane, cocking the left wrist, turning the hips as fast as possible, focusing on supination, bracing the right side, maintaining adhesion of the arms, manipulating the left forearm, taking shallow divots, etc. These alone could keep you busy building a lousy golf swing for the next decade – unless you have the talent, time, and inclination to pound a thousand balls or so, and have the dedication to do it again the next day, and the next, and the next.

Where Hogan ended up in his quest, with the answers he was looking for all along, no doubt convinced him that all the activity that went before was spent grooving a faulty swing. For him it was also likely unavoidable, but we can avoid much of the trouble by focusing, as Hogan recommended, on the true fundamentals.

I have given you part of the revelation about Henny Bogan, which is not exactly a "big teaser." After all, Hogan had a nameplate on his desk given to him by his employees that read "Henny Bogan," according to his wife Valerie's account in Martin Davis' book *Ben Hogan: The Man Behind the Mystique*. But, outside of offhand references to Henny Bogan sprinkled throughout the Hogan storyline, or Hogan's word or references, there is nothing to explain the link

Introduction

between them other than Valerie Hogan's words. It would be easy to dismiss the context as a "lark" perhaps. But Hogan was a man who was not, from all reports, very "larky." I always thought there was more here to explain than a mere "lark." I trust that in the final analysis you will agree.

CHAPTER ONE

Desperate Times Lead to Desperate Measures

"It's up to the player to dig it out on the practice tee by himself through trial and error. You can't do it in five minutes; you're lucky if you can do it in five years. It's a training process. Give it enough time and thought, anybody can break 80."
Ben Hogan

In the spring of 1946 a golfer driven to desperation by a recurring hooking problem, which he described as akin to having a "rattlesnake" in his golf bag, reached the end of his proverbial rope. He took two or three weeks off from the pro tour and did not touch a club for several days. He had been fighting the hooking problem with swing tips, quick fixes, dogmatic routines and "bromides" of one sort or another for the better part of his adult life and through two very distinct periods of his golf career. But he had never quite grasped the measure of the problem.

The issue dogged him every step of the way, including the time period after he turned professional at age seventeen and joined the pro tour in 1932 at age nineteen, and continuing until 1938. He made some swing adjustments that year that kept the problem relatively at bay for a good period of time. He rode those modifications through World War II and his time in the Army Air Corps, and after his release from service up to early 1946. The dogmatic practice, the adjustments, and the tinkering of his swing were not really new or different than his established pattern throughout his golfing career and would continue until he was no longer able to sustain the regimen. The significance of this instance in the spring of 1946, in comparison to all the other years of trial and practice, was the self-realization that after striving to be great from 1932-46, he was not "cutting it." He had not won the big tournaments and he still suffered from problems that plagued him as a rookie in 1932, predominantly his tendency to hook the ball, but also his inability to control the ball and to hit it high or low, right or left on demand.

A golfer of lesser aspirations, standards, desire, and drive would have soldiered on with swing fixes and swing tips, content to make a decent living, while resigning himself to somewhat lesser results than he had set out to achieve. But not this golfer. This golfer wanted to win major championships and play a style of golf that would give him a chance to win every time he teed up the ball. It wasn't a simple matter of playing better by shooting lower scores that motivated him. He wanted total mastery over the golf ball, to be able to draw it by hitting it from right to left or to fade it by hitting it left to right, when and where he wanted to, to meet whatever demands the shot dictated at that moment. He wanted to have the type of swing that enabled him to manipulate the ball as if it was on a string he controlled, to hit it high or low, and be in command of the flight trajectory of the golf ball. He quite simply wanted to be the best golfer in the world and the greatest golfer of all time. He believed that was within his grasp.

This golfer can be none other than the legendary William Ben Hogan, known more simply to golf fans as Ben Hogan. Hindsight makes it somewhat easier to make sense of or to understand how he came to this desperate state, but those around him at the time were unaware of his turmoil, his motivations, or the rationale that drove him to pursue what seemed to most as inexplicable, dogmatic practice routines. He achieved a good measure of success from 1938-46, averaging about twenty professional golf tournaments a year (excluding the war years), winning twenty-two Professional Golf Association (PGA) tournament events as well as the first two of his Vardon Trophies, the award given to the professional golfer with the lowest scoring average on the professional tour. He was the leading money winner on the tour three years in a row. Even by golf standards more than a half-century later, that would be considered a good professional golf career, certainly good enough to earn him a spot in the top thirty of all-time PGA Tour winners, and ahead of a number of very good golfers such as Greg Norman. But he had not won a major; it remained an elusive goal and an exclusive fraternity that did not number him as a member. The lack of a major on his resume marked him as the "best player never to have won a major" and also made problematic any post-golf accolades. This issue represented a powerful, smoldering motivation for Hogan, like an itch that could not be reached or a task long deferred.

Winning a major title would validate Hogan's status as a top-notch golfer and eliminate the burning in his gut that motivated him. Hogan was singularly driven by the relentless pursuit of a higher standard representing his own goals, desires, and aspirations. He often commented that he was the sole judge of his standards. He deeply believed there was a way to master the swing and achieve mastery over the golf ball and, throughout this period, he sensed he was on the right track. His tenacious pursuit of a solution continued for years, undeterred by short-term setbacks or challenges. He kept the faith that he would achieve it right up to that fateful spring of 1946.

Hogan committed to outwork the other professional golfers early on. He first established and later, as a byproduct of his success, legitimized the discipline of practice among his fellow professionals, who were slow to warm to the idea. Hogan was a "belt and suspenders" guy from the standpoint of practice routines. If other pros worked on a particular shot or technique for an hour or two, Hogan worked on the same technique for a week or until he "owned it." He first mastered the basic shot and then worked to master variations of the theme: to hit it high and low; draw, fade, and hit it out of sand; from rough, good and bad lies, and all variations he might encounter on the golf course. He wanted to hit the shot perfectly during practice before he faced a similar situation on the golf course.

Hogan built confidence through his practice regimen, the type of confidence that comes from knowing that he had outworked all the other golfers and left no stone unturned toward that end. Hogan would later say that there are three ways to beat a person; you outwork them, you outthink them and, if that doesn't work, you intimidate them. He likely never hit a shot in a tournament that he hadn't practiced exhaustively beforehand. In practical terms, that meant a training regimen of hitting golf balls from sunup to sundown, six hundred to a thousand golf balls a day when he wasn't playing in tournaments. When he was scheduled to play professional golf tournaments he was the first golfer to arrive at the practice tee before the round, and the last to depart afterwards. Only the setting sun drove him away from the practice tee. Champion golfer Gene Sarazen observed that he felt Hogan often left his best golf on the practice tee during these years, while also noting that he found Hogan's routine "physically and mentally exhausting." Hogan famously observed during this time period that the only thing a golfer really needed was "more daylight." He practiced putting and chipping in his hotel room at night to the point where his fellow golfers added a caveat to their hotel room criterion: any room not next to Hogan.

Hogan lived in Fort Worth, Texas, throughout much of his life and he hit balls year round. In fact, he often said he never took time off and that he enjoyed every minute of practice. He also opined, "Every day of practice that you miss will take you a day longer to get better." His peers and friends alike were sometimes derisive in describing his regimen, and bewildered at the need for so much practice. In fact, the very notion of hitting practice shots *after* a round was thought preposterous, like locking the barn door after the horse ran away. Professional golfers of Hogan's early days on tour rarely hit golf balls to practice other than to warm up before a round, and none of the best players on the pro tour hit golf balls after a round. While this may be attributed somewhat to traditions dating back to the use of hickory shafts (hand-picked and often accrued one by one to complete a set, they were not as hardy and therefore could not withstand such intensive use as the steel shafts that predominated in Hogan's time), Hogan was the sole practitioner of this methodology until late in his career. For those inclined to think about and be impressed with numbers, a conservative estimate works out to something like a bit over three million golf balls from his turning professional in 1932 until 1946, assuming that he took a month off throughout the year. Most reports and his own words indicate that he didn't.

Despite possessing by the spring of 1946 what should have been a very mature swing and a consistent routine that by all accounts was producing high-quality results, Hogan remained somewhat short of his standards. After the 1946 Masters Tournament he hit the wall for at least the fourth time in his professional career. With all the books about Hogan's life, his later successes and the infamy of his secret, the early periods of his career and his struggles remain somewhat of a footnote in most accounts, the details subordinate in comparison to the focus on the later period of his career. That is understandable, as he only played in twenty tournaments from 1932-37, which was fewer than he would later average each year. He played half of that total in 1937. A summary of his results during that time period shows that he won less than fifteen hundred dollars and he returned home three times after going broke. This first part of his career could be called "the optimist and construction stage," as Hogan found that he could not compete with the other pros. But it did not deter him.

An important point that is often lost in describing this early period is why Hogan turned professional so young and while so relatively "green" that he did poorly on the tour. The answer is quite simple: He reached the age of seventeen and was no longer welcome to caddy at Glen Garden Country Club. He was expected to move on to bigger and better things, such as college or a serious job. Only one caddy was selected to continue an association with the club beyond the maximum age of seventeen, and that golfer was Byron Nelson. Hogan had no such options, nor the money for college. In fact, he dropped out of school and he had nothing to lose by immediately starting on his life's choice of career, despite knowing he had so much to learn.

Hogan methodically went about incorporating myriad changes to his swing and his game a piece at a time, like building a house, until he could compete with the other pros. He was mature beyond his years in the manner with which he went about a self-assessment of his golf swing. He was even more adept in deciding upon the elements to integrate into his game. He was not above copying the successful pros of his day, and many of the techniques that became the bedrock of his swing were copied directly and unashamedly from the professional golfers he played with and against. Such mimicry or flattery in its most sincere form was somewhat of a tradition prior to the advent of the modern-day "swing gurus." Most of the pro golfers were club pros that made a good part of their living teaching at their home clubs. It was extremely rare for golfers to support themselves solely from their tournament winnings and only the top golfers could do so.

Hogan's taste of the sting of desperation happened on three separate occasions during this "first stage" prior to 1938. Each of his attempts at the professional tour (1931, 1932, and 1934) ended the same way, with Hogan broke and forced to return to Fort Worth to take on odd jobs to save money for his next attempt. They were not particularly great jobs, including a stint as a dealer in a casino where he came in contact with a number of unsavory characters. Ft. Worth was a rough-and-tumble western town in the 1920-30s. Hogan simply did not have the game, temperament or skills to make a living during this first stage of his career.

What I refer to as the "second (or defensive) stage" of his career encompassed the period starting with his tasting desperation a fourth time. He was on the verge of going broke again, down to eighty-six dollars, when his tires were stolen at the Oakland Open in January 1938. He steeled his resolve and managed a sixth-place finish and winnings of $286 under the most acute pressure imaginable – the sort Lee Trevino spoke of where you are playing for money you don't have in your pocket, against people with no sense of humor.

Hogan was playing for his life's aspiration and everything he had worked for since 1932. Now married, he and his wife Valerie had been surviving on hamburgers and oranges for weeks to save enough money to get to the next event. Oakland marked a breakthrough of sorts and, as it turned out, signaled the end of his struggles and the beginning of an amazing run of momentum that saw Hogan set a record by finishing in the money over one hundred straight times that carried through World War II.

The pro tour only paid the top ten finishers in most tournaments, with the lower finishers making just short of what was needed to cover the expenses of even those prone to frugal living. Good and consistent golf was mandatory to survive on tour in those early days. Hogan was able to augment his income at times with the odd outing with amateurs or by winning prize money offered for things such as long-drive contests. This stage of his career is characterized by Hogan executing all manner of fundamental tips and techniques to suppress his tendency to hook the ball, to compensate for his inability to hit the ball on a higher trajectory, and to deal with his inability to fade or to hit the ball with a left to right ball flight. These efforts culminated in several changes to his golf swing that became increasingly important to Hogan's emerging consistency, including: fixing his tendency to regrip the club at the top of the back swing based on a tip from Harry "Lighthorse" Cooper, weakening his grip based on a tip from Henry Picard, the eventual discovery of the importance of the swing plane, and a dogmatic approach to golf course management.

The defensive stage of his career was obviously a remarkable stretch of golf in comparison with the first stage. But his struggles with the problem of hooking the golf ball, coupled with his inability to hit the ball as high as he wanted to, continuously surfaced in the years before the war. He did not win any majors and he hit the "desperation wall" again for a fifth time after being released from the service in 1945 and discovering that his old hooking problem, the "rattlesnake," was waiting for him in spite of all the work on his game during the War years.

His five wins and fourteen top ten finishes in 1945 included three wins in a row in a single month and would have been a cause for great celebration for most golfers. A closer look at the record reveals that Hogan finished in the top three places in twelve tournaments in 1945 and the campaign could have been significantly better had he not, in his own words, "frittered tournaments away." Hogan knew better than anybody that his old nemesis, the hook, was back, and it cost him dearly during the 1945 season. The defensive stage continued through the Masters Tournament of 1946, when Hogan became desperate for the fifth and final time of his professional career after three putting the final green from inside of ten feet to finish second by a shot. He was determined to figure out a cure for his hooking problems once and for all in order to arrive at the final or seventy-second hole with an insurmountable lead. He later discussed this timeframe in an interview with Ken Venturi, noting that his hooking problem was so acute at times that he was unable to get a four-wood up in the air.

The stage of his career starting with the post-Masters timeframe in 1946 and his win at the inaugaural Colonial National Invitational Tournament, Fort Worth, run by lifelong friend and sponsor Marvin Leonard, is simply the "breakthrough" stage and there is no better evidence of him solving his hooking problems than to look at the record and contrast it with those earlier years. From January 1946 to January 1949, Hogan won thirty-two tournaments, three major championships, a third Vardon trophy, and he was the leading money-winner twice more and voted PGA Player of the Year for the first time. More important perhaps to Hogan, he was acknowledged as the best player in the world, replacing his Glen Garden Country Club, caddy yard friend and fellow Fort Worth resident, Byron Nelson. Byron had retired from golf in 1946 at the peak of his career with his title of "Mr. Golf" intact, a moniker earned through his glorious play during the War years and beyond, including his phenomenal run of winning eleven professional golf tournaments in a row and a total of eighteen tournaments in 1945. The title of "Mr. Golf" was somewhat grudgingly accorded to Hogan sometime after Byron's retirement, although he was truthfully nowhere near as popular a figure with the fans, tournament organizers, or golf writers as was the affable Nelson. Hogan averaged twenty-seven professional tournaments a year during the breakthrough stage and probably would have continued playing at that rate for some time to come, as he played championship level golf well into his fifties.

The car accident on 2 February 1949 changed all that and we are left to ponder what might have been had a healthy Hogan continued at the pace and success rate he established. Hogan was thirty-six years old at the time of the accident, and at the top of the game. Rumors of his retirement had circulated for some time after the War, with some wondering what he was trying to prove by continuing to play at such a frenetic pace. The travel was getting to him and Valerie, particularly the long drives. But in truth he was still relatively "fresh" from a golf standpoint, despite the constant struggle to fix his swing and his relative seniority.

Hogan played the tour sporadically starting in 1932 and pretty much full time from 1937-42 and from 1945-49, with the break for World War II factored out. But germane to the issue of freshness, Hogan had only just found his game in April-May of 1946 and he still had the proverbial skip in his step associated with his breakthrough. No less an authority than Byron Nelson, who knew Hogan better than most others, was quoted as saying that he was puzzled over what Hogan was still trying to prove. In spite of his somewhat deserved reputation as "a hard case," with all the secrecy and mystique notwithstanding, Hogan was not that hard to figure out. He aspired to be the greatest golfer of all time and he had just found his pace.

So he was barely thirty-four months into the breakthrough stage when fate dictated that Hogan return to square one again, and enter in February 1949 the fourth or "optimism and reclamation" stage of his career. Doctors were not sure he would ever walk again after the accident, never mind play golf. The head-on collision with a Greyhound bus resulted in a fractured collarbone, a broken pelvis, a snapped left ankle, a somewhat mangled left leg, a broken rib, as well as damaged and bruised organs. He almost lost his left eye and eventually had to have his femoral artery tied off to prevent blood clots from reaching his heart. This procedure was fraught with risk, as vascular surgery was in its relative infancy in the 1940s. Recovery was problematic and for a long time there was talk of amputating his left leg. The circulation to his lower limbs was forever degraded to the point where he was forced into a regimen consisting of Epson salts baths and liniments to control swelling before and after play.

Nobody would have been surprised if it turned out that Hogan could no longer play golf, let alone compete at the championship level. But this was Ben Hogan and, remarkably, he played championship golf again only eleven months after the accident, tying for first place at the Los Angeles Open and losing in a playoff to Sam Snead the following day. Hogan astoundingly won the United States Open Championship (U.S. Open) in a playoff at Merion Golf Club in Philadelphia later that summer, about seventeen months after his accident. The 1950 U.S. Open Championship still included "Open Saturday," with thirty-six holes of play on one day deciding the outcome. He tied for the lead with a par on the final hole, with an approach shot that was memorialized for all time by photographer Hy Peskin. Hogan won the playoff the next day over Lloyd Mangrum and George Fazio. His achievement that week on a very tough golf course in the thick of the summer heat was simply remarkable and a testimony to his strength, determination, drive, and desire. His play after his accident fostered a mixture of empathy, respect and warmth from many fans who had been less appreciative if not downright hostile toward his perceived aloofness in the not so distant past. Hogan noticed and responded as best he could to this change in attitude toward him, fostering a relationship that remained somewhat short of affection. Even his second-most-persistent nemesis (behind his hooking), the press, seemed to have granted him some grudging dispensation in light of the struggles he endured to compete on the pro tour.

Despite the successes and his newfound status, Hogan was truly only a shadow of his former "iron man" self from then on. He never played more than nine tournaments a year and averaged six, which left him far short of meeting the PGA tour minimum rounds required to qualify for awards such as the Vardon Trophy (for lowest scoring average on tour). He put up a remarkable standard when he did play, winning ten more tournaments, including six major championships, winning the PGA Player of The Year three more times and voted the Professional Sports Athlete of the Year in 1953. His 1953 season, in which he won five of six pro tournaments he entered, including the Masters, the U.S. Open and the Open (British) Championships, was the second-greatest golf campaign of all time, just behind Byron Nelson's 1945 season when Byron won eleven tournaments in a row and eighteen overall in what may be the greatest sports season ever for a golfer or any athlete (Some question the level of competition during Byron's phenomenal run, it being the post-war years and such.)

Hogan could not compete in the 1953 PGA Championship because the golf scheduling bodies of the day were arrogant enough that they did not routinely deconflict the championship schedules, and the British and PGA schedules conflicted. Hogan had played infrequently in the PGA anyway, because of his dislike of the format and its multiple opportunities to play thirty-six holes of golf in a single day. The Open required golfers to qualify and even the winner had difficulty covering travel expenses. Winning the Open Championship at Carnoustie in his only try is the stuff of legends. He had to qualify for the tournament like any other golfer. His victory is still fresh in the minds of the British golfing public, despite the passage of more than half a century.

The final or fifth stage of Hogan's career from 1950 forward could aptly be referred to as "the fulfillment or vindication" stage. In the words of many of his peers, he was the standard against which other golfers were measured. He was hands-down the best ball striker in any tournament he played from 1950 through 1970. Fellow pros watched him practice and often returned to the course to walk in his gallery after completion of their rounds. He had amazing control of the golf ball and moved it at will. He played championship-caliber golf well into his fifties, including a record-setting back-nine score of 30 in the third round of his final Masters in 1967 at age fifty-four, finishing in the top ten. He might have won several dozen or more tournaments were it not for the deteriorating condition of his left (dominant) eye that made him the worst putter in the field each time he teed it up. For example, he was paired at age forty-seven with amateur Jack Nicklaus for the final thirty-six holes at the U.S. Open Championship of 1960 at Cherry Hills in Denver, Colorado. Hogan was in contention until he pressed to make birdie on the 17th hole, knowing he needed to hit it absolutely stiff to have any chance of making a putt. His ball found the green but drew back into the water, dashing his hopes for a record-breaking fifth championship. Nicklaus later observed that if he had putted for Hogan, he would have won by ten shots (Hogan famously commented that if amateur Nicklaus had a brain in his head, he would have won by ten shots. Nicklaus agreed, with no animosity intended or taken.)

Impressions, folklore, and stories linger and abound about Hogan. Some who don't know the Hogan story tend to think that he was somewhat of an overnight success or that he suddenly came out of nowhere and started to win everything he entered; or that he was a bad golfer who all of a sudden discovered something that made him into a great golfer, with a connotation that the same could happen to you or me, or to any golf hack who knew his "secret." Some believe Hogan was much better after his accident and that it somehow transformed him into some type of "golf automaton" who was not quite human. Others view tape or video of Hogan in his advanced years and draw conclusions and develop theories about his technique that are somewhat analogous to attempting to learn pitching secrets by watching a veteran baseball pitcher, who can no longer throw the fastball, survive on the curve and knuckleball. Still others believe of his secret that Hogan was "taking us for a ride," although they offer no explanation for his dramatic success after 1946. More believe that Hogan may have found something, but it is no longer relevant with the advent of technology in golf clubs and golf balls that have canceled out any advantage in technique.

In summer 2009, a story circulated on the Internet about how, shortly before his death, Hogan told noted golf psychologist Bob Ratella that pronation was not his secret and that it was just what he told people because they wanted to hear something specific. Some believe there is a hidden meaning or context in *Five Lessons* that can only be deciphered if approached from a set of assumptions that have not yet been made clear (to anybody). Others have reportedly been given Hogan's secret either directly or through a third party; however, many of these "tips" turned out to be fundamentals covered in *Five Lessons*. The folklore surrounding Hogan has not abated with his passing or the intervening years.

CHAPTER TWO

Guess My Secret

"The secret is in the dirt."
Ben Hogan

The details of the breakthrough Hogan achieved on that spring morning shortly after the Masters in 1946 is the one bit of unfinished business that might put all the other information into context. Hogan himself said that he "had found a secret" and he described it as such in conversations from that point forward. The topic gained interest and momentum as Hogan piled up wins, culminating with speculation in *Life* magazine (5 April 1954) by the top pros of the day explaining their theories. Hogan later "revealed" the secret in the 8 August 1955 issue of *Life*.

The matter could have been put to bed thereafter except for a few small details. One of the biggest issues or problems, according to the secret theorists, is that Hogan failed to make mention of the secret in either the series of golf lessons published in *Sports Illustrated* in the spring of 1957 or the book that resulted from the articles and published later that fall, *Five Lessons: The Modern Fundamentals of Golf*. That supposed "glaring omission" renewed debate on the topic and raised anew the belief that Hogan had not quite told all he knew or that he was somehow withholding or manipulating information. The issue of withholding information gained credence, found a ready audience, and was easily propagated. Further, many golfers who flocked to his instruction manual and adopted the fundamental techniques outlined in *Five Lessons* discovered to their chagrin that their golf did not improve; in fact, many became worse than ever before. Many had difficulty with a number of the aspects touted, including the relatively weakened grip and the concept of the swing plane.

Golf instructors and even his fellow pros insinuated that there must be more to it than Hogan had acknowledged and many disputed the very fundamentals outlined in *Five Lessons*, in particular the relatively weak grip and what was interpreted by many as advocacy for an overly flat swing plane. Golfers found that the weakened grip caused them to slice more than ever and, for those prone to hook, the inside move advocated therein made them hook the ball even more. The concept of the swing plane with two different swing paths, executed under a pane of glass, was a bit too esoteric for most golfers. Many instructors dismissed the concept as advocating a swing plane that was "too flat," despite Hogan's admonition that such broad-based assumptions without deeper analysis were part of the problem hindering improved golf. With the advent of television and the exposure of golf on an increasingly larger scale, the emerging "modern" golf swings of the late 1950 and 1960s, by the best and most popular professional golfers, were available for public viewing and were quite dissimilar (with the exception of Gary Player) to the swing fundamentals advocated in *Five Lessons*.

Hogan himself was somewhat silent on the controversy, while maintaining that "everything" he knew about the fundamentals, the full golf swing, was in there (e.g., *Five Lessons*). He reaffirmed that sentiment during a 1984 interview with Nick Seitz of *Golf Magazine* that was subsequently added as a foreword to *Five Lessons*, stating that he would write it the same way nearly thirty years later. Hogan did go into somewhat greater detail during the interview about his efforts to cure his hook problem by incorporating pronation in his swing, but he closed with the admonition that he would write the book the same way and not change a word. He also stated that the golf fundamentals had not changed with the passage of time, the advent and refinement of technology, or with improvements in course maintenance.

The lingering idea or notion of some unrevealed secret or technique should have been put to bed once and for all (again). The go-for-broke or heroic playing style and the swing trends of the 1960s, including the technique of swinging in a manner that was labeled a reverse "C" and would lead to back and other medical problems for its practitioners, eventually fell into disfavor and there was somewhat of a resurgence of golfers advocating a more fundamental approach that sought clarity in Hogan's technique. However, rumors began to circulate anew about other secrets, and Hogan himself later spoke of secrets that had not been previously revealed. Speculation built around a technique that would enable pros to shoot in the fifties, accompanied by a rumor that Hogan wanted one hundred thousand dollars to reveal the secret. Many again picked up on the notion that there was a "real secret," after all.

Some combination of factors resulted in a breakdown of the negotiations that prevented whatever information might have been available from seeing the light of day, with the "usual" mystery of whether Hogan had ever really been part of the effort in the first place. Hogan never did reveal any additional information, leaving others to ponder and speculate as to whether he had been forthright with the *Life* article in the first place, or if there was some other secret move or information that he alone found that allowed him to achieve such mastery over the golf ball.

Those who watched and played with him over the years regarded him as the greatest ball striker of all time. He remains a huge influence on the game with the passage of years and his legend, or more appropriately, his mystique, has only increased. The only thing that keeps Hogan from being considered the greatest golfer of all time is the record because, in the final analysis, we judge golfers by their records of wins and major championships. The debate over the greatest golfer of all time is an interesting standpoint from which to lament what might have been for Hogan. But the same could be said truthfully of Bobby Jones, who retired as an amateur and never did turn professional, or even Byron Nelson, had he not retired early in 1946 at age thirty-three. The golf standard is applied in a somewhat capricious manner when it comes to these matters or Sam Snead would be the greatest based on wins alone, in spite of the "blight" on his resume representing his failure to win the U.S. Open Championship.

Long before the *Life* articles in 1954-55, Hogan simply stated that he discovered a secret that saved at least a stroke a round. The secret allowed him to erect a huge "wall" down the left side of the golf course that he was supremely confident he would not go beyond. Was it the secret he revealed in the *Life* magazine article? If so, why did the effort to reveal something else some thirty-odd years later gain momentum?

Despite loose reporting that sometimes walks a fine line with the facts, nobody ever questioned Hogan's honesty or doubted that he was a man with a deep abiding sense of honor, righteousness, and integrity. He had a reputation as a man who "did the right thing," and he lived that way. There are dozens of anecdotes supporting his reputation in this regard, none of which are more poignant than the story of the first batch of clubs produced in 1954 by the new Ben Hogan Golf Company. Hogan inspected each and every club and decided they were inferior products. He ordered them scrapped. His partner did not agree, believing they should be reused somehow or sold much like seconds. Hogan would not budge and eventually bought out his partner. He scrapped one hundred thousand dollars worth of clubs and had to seek additional capital to fund the next production run.

The notion that he was stringing "us" along somehow and that he either didn't discover something or he was somehow playing with the public just does not square with the facts of his life. Johnny Miller famously observed that Hogan often spoke in parables, in a style that Miller likened to the *Bible*. I believe that observation to be the most germane in terms of attempting to understand Hogan's words over the years. Toward that end I think it is instructive to give serious consideration to Miller's assessment and look at some of Hogan's own words and sayings that provide clues and an indication of what he felt was important to know and share. People often say he was a man of few words and he chose them carefully. Yet the collective "we" are often somewhat dismissive of those very words or thoughts without giving them the type of deliberation warranted in consideration of them coming not from a good golfer or from some swing guru who never won a thing in his life, but from the man roundly acknowledged as the greatest ball striker the game has ever seen.

I read a more recent review of *Five Lessons* by an author of golf books who basically described *Five Lessons* as overrated! Can you imagine? Separately, some well-known golf instructors have somehow found a reverse pivot in Hogan's swing, while still others have insinuated that Hogan thought he was doing things in his swing that he was not really doing. A charitable view of these observations suggests that the shadow of the unknown in the form of the secret confuses the layman and the professional alike. But if Ben Hogan was hitting a shot of some difficulty that required him to execute what looks in a still picture like a reverse pivot, you can bet the bank that there was some shot he was preparing for or something he was doing that mandated it and there was no other way to pull the shot off!

The path to figuring out what Hogan discovered, and what else there was to reveal that he may not have shared, must clearly run like a thread through his statements and documented remarks. Many writers, historians, and reporters alike touch on Hogan's effort to improve his game, without answering basic questions about the nature of his quest. Hogan himself was somewhat dismissive of questions about his training regimen, simply stating that early in his career his swing was "awful" and he therefore needed all that practice. That factor may account for his actions in the first stage of his career through early 1938 and a good bit of the early second stage, as well. For the second stage, I termed it a defensive stage because I believe Hogan did about everything in his power to avoid hooking the ball by making major adjustments to his clubs, weakening his grip, changing his swing path, and working on his release. We know Hogan had a hooking problem, but even a cursory or surface review of his own instructional materials is sufficient to confirm that a hook is a *symptom* of a problem and not the problem to fix, per se. And that fixing a hook without working on the underlying source of the problem can lead to other problems or even defer to a later time the actual fix needed to resolve the issue.

We know Hogan spent most of this earlier time period working to cure his hooking problem, but what was the actual root of the problem? What was it that caused Hogan to hook the ball in the first place? Why didn't he simply stop doing it or change whatever it was that was causing him to hook? He clearly understood the fundamentals of the golf swing by this time as well if not better than any golfer who ever lived.

There is an anecdote about an exchange between Hogan and a German golf instructor who was insulted by Hogan's apparent questioning of his bona fides because he asked about the cause of a hook in the golf swing. Hogan's retort was basically that any pro worth his salt knew what caused a hook, to which the German pro, initially somewhat insulted, eventually was forced to agree. Now what about the gander?

We know by Hogan's own words that by 1938 he knew all the elements required to produce a proper golf swing, but he also stated that the information was less well integrated than it later became. Many assume this referred to whatever information he added or dug out of the dirt in 1946 that allowed him to finally put the swing together in a manner that solved his hook problem. Others assumed he was referring to the fundamentals he outlined in his series of *Sports Illustrated* articles that were later published as *Five Lessons*. Or was he referring to the *Life* articles that addressed his secret directly? He published *Power Golf* in 1948, and it is fairly easy to discern the differences between it and *Five Lessons*, for instance, the grip, the stance, and the plane, to name a few, with the latter presenting a more nuanced and refined treatment of the golf-swing fundamentals.

This problem of getting to the bottom line or the base truth on this and other issues has long complicated Hogan's story, never more so than in the years since his passing in 1997. There are as many variations of Hogan lore as ever, and new information is added to the pile by the month. Hogan's lingering reputation for mystery, secrecy, single-sentence answers to complex questions, and his tendency to talk in parables, as put forth by Johnny Miller, continues to obfuscate even simple issues related to his story. Ben Crenshaw wrote how Hogan often took to deep thought before he answered a question, even seemingly simple questions that could apparently be readily or easily answered. For instance, Texans have a reputation as good wind players and fellow Texan, Crenshaw, asked Hogan what he did to hit the ball low to keep it under the wind. Hogan paused, looked down and thought for a long time about this apparent softball question, to the point of making it uncomfortable for those waiting for an answer. He finally replied that he tried to "hit it on the second groove." Crenshaw, obviously a championship golfer in his own right, was quite happy with that answer. But I've read other accounts of this story where the reporter (or writer) took issue somehow and was dismissive of Hogan's answer as being cryptic, esoteric, odd in some unexplained manner, secretive, or mysterious. As an aside, it is interesting to note that "Pipeline" Moe Norman, who may be the straightest hitter of a golf ball of all time and the exception to Hogan's observation that a straight ball is an accident, often observed that he hit it so straight by hitting it on "the second groove."

In context with Miller's observation, Hogan was answering questions from a particular perspective, set of assumptions, and viewpoint. I believe that view was from the standpoint of Hogan's actual technique, which he had to "translate" in order for it to be usable for other golfers. Hogan went to great lengths in these situations to ensure that he was providing an accurate answer of what it "felt like" in consideration of his actual technique for his swing, translated into what it would feel like for a "normal" golfer in the vernacular used in his outline of the fundamentals described in *Five Lessons*.

What is the difference? His answer to Ben Crenshaw, for instance, could have been along the lines of taking his backswing but particularly his hands, and therefore his pronation move, deeper and lower in somewhat of a delayed backswing, delaying his turn in both directions as well as his release by releasing the hands or supinating somewhat low and late, while staying somewhat flat-footed or on his right side longer, and hitting the ball in a manner that produced a shallow or no divot at all while still pulling aggressively with the left side. It is far easier to put all that Hogan swing-specific, technical detail and jargon into a simplified answer useable by the average gofler that tracks with the elegant simplicity of *Five Lessons*, to wit: "I try to hit it on the second groove." His attempts to reduce the body of knowledge he possessed to sound bites and one-liners was challenging at best, since he spent a lifetime perfecting compensations that worked for his unique swing.

Despite Hogan's reputation as a relatively dogmatic person who has at times been uncharitably described as "not giving a hoot about others," I believe this to be one of many examples providing direct evidence that he was keenly aware of the potential ramifications of his words. In fact he cared enough about the subject that he conscientiously attempted to guard against giving people golf tips and advice that would prove ruinous if implemented out of context. Such was his reputation that he famously responded, "Something wrong with your arm?" to a golfer who asked if there was something he should work on after playing a PGA practice round with the legend. Gardiner Dickinson was later referred to as "Mini-hawk," as he copied everything about Hogan down to the hat. Dickinson spent the better part of a year working on his "arm problem," only to discover that he had been working on the wrong arm! So Hogan's reticence was as much pragmatic as it was a personal preference. Many are those whose attempts to mimic his swing or technique proved disastrous.

A landmark scientific study effort was supported by The Golf Society of

Great Britain to document the fundamentals of the golf swing. Published in 1968, *The Search for the Perfect Swing* produced a working model of the golf swing and tested that model through computer "calculations" or simulations that tested the hypothesis postulating the interrelationships of the mechanical elements. The scientists depicted the working model as a hinged lever that represented the ideal swing. Hogan's swing sequence in the book is a near match for the ideal swing model, although the scientists increasingly focused on a simpler single hinge and lever, rather than the more complex human two-armed swing with its multiple levers, hinges, and multi-dimensional shifting plane(s). Further, the scientists commented that Hogan's swing exhibited and therefore matched so many of the attributes defining the model that scientists could have used it in every chapter as the exemplar or human version of the model!

I am convinced that Hogan had a secret that he executed or, more appropriately, a technique that allowed him to resolve his problems with hooking the ball once and for all. He told us what it was in *Life* magazine in 1955. It was pronation, and as Jackie Burke Jr. once observed and Jim Mclean stated, it was also a specific subset out of the little details or the hundred fundamentals he was working on at any one time. He built them one after the other, like a chess variation, while testing their integration within his swing through trial and error and practice. He did not put pronation in *Five Lessons* simply because he did not consider it necessary or a fundamental of a proper swing, per se, but more along the lines of a technique to compensate for a swing flaw.

So what does that leave from the standpoint of a secret? The remaining piece of information he did not tell us is how he discovered the secret or the technique he employed to discover that it worked. A natural reaction to that last statement by those who know the story is: Aha, but of course he did! He explained that he took two or three weeks off, did not touch a club for two or three days, woke up one morning and thought about the old Scottish technique of pronation, and it worked immediately. Case closed!

I think the latter part of that description is the only piece of the story that is not quite true: that it worked immediately. More to the point, I think it worked immediately, but Hogan did not realize it (immediately). There is a reason for that. The reason, as well as the implications, is really the only remaining secrets to be disclosed in this enduring mystery that has lasted since the spring of 1946. I suspect that you may initially be surprised to read about it, but shortly thereafter you will come to a belly laugh over the irony and silliness engendered in all the speculation and stories over the years.

Interestingly enough, Hogan and Jack Nicklaus share the same ball-striking philosophy, in spite of the obvious differences in their swings. Nicklaus has always been a lot more forthcoming in describing his technique. His instructor, Jack Grout, played the pro tour and was close with Hogan in the 1930s when they traveled for a time together. Grout benefitted greatly from his own struggles and also from watching the young Hogan mature as a golfer over the course of that decade, including his struggles to tame the "rattlesnake."

So the key and clues to his secret are in his words, and the answer should be congruent with his statements over the years. There is no lack of sayings, slogans, and "Hoganisms" to sort through; but careful scrutiny reveals a first order of statements that should be addressed, as they are linked via a theme that runs like a thread through each. These statements are similar to dominoes, the fall or solving of which enable each of their brethren to take their place in the puzzle, or to facilitate the drop of their neighbor.

For example, Hogan often stated that he knew all the fundamental elements of the golf swing by 1938, but the information was less well integrated than it later became. Many assume this statement refers to the difference in information between his books *Power Golf* and *Five Lessons* – with the latter representing a more integrated treatment or perhaps more context, a cleanup of sorts of the fundamentals that had changed as presented in *Power Golf*. Part of the problem or challenge in sorting through this detail is that *Power Golf* was published in 1948, at least two years after Hogan discovered his secret, yet the book does not show evidence of thought influenced by that event. That thereby dates the information in *Power Golf* as reflective of the non-integrated stage of Hogan's development prior to 1946. I think the context of Hogan's statement is more easily understood in light of two other comments he made. One is the fairly well-known statement that if you do the opposite of what the body wants to do or the opposite of the body's natural tendency, you will probably end up with a pretty good golf swing. This and previously mentioned statements absolutely meet the criterion or assessment made by Johnny Miller about Hogan speaking in parables. But there is no more curious statement made by Hogan than his revelation in *Five*

Lessons that he realized all of a sudden in 1946: "There was no practical reason for me to feel I might suddenly 'lose it all.' I would guess that what lay behind my new confidence was this: I had stopped trying to do a great many difficult things perfectly because it had become clear in my mind that this ambitious over-thoroughness was neither possible nor advisable, or even necessary."

Taken at face value, one would have to believe that a man who spent the better part of fourteen years hitting more than three million golf balls in an attempt to master his swing, and do away with his hook, suddenly awoke one day and realized he simply didn't need to do that any longer. Could it have taken him fourteen years to come to that conclusion, or is this thought linked somehow more appropriately to the fact that what he found that spring morning in 1946 was the final piece that allowed him to integrate all the pieces and parts of the swing he had been working on that prevented him hooking? What he discovered allowed him to stop all the defensive moves once and for all, since he solved his problem through simpler means. In keeping with the theme of parables, Hogan often said his secret was easy to spot if you knew – or he told you – where to look. Most have assumed that he meant his wrist in the wake of the *Life* magazine articles. Recent theorists have us looking to other places, including his arm(s), his leg (right), his backswing (angle), his head lowering several inches during his swing, or in his follow-through. There may be no better example of Hogan's words as parable or greater evidence of his sense of humor than his statement regarding this topic, as he meant in his head! Many of those statements were made before the *Life* magazine articles were released and they took on somewhat of a different meaning after the articles were published.

After Hogan was beaten in a great upset by relatively unheralded Jack Fleck in the playoff for the 1955 U.S. Open Championship, writers asked Hogan if Fleck had beaten him by using a secret, which in and of itself is indicative of the somewhat uneasy relationship Hogan maintained with reporters. Hogan replied, "Fleck may have used a secret, but it was not *my* secret." These statements are best understood in hindsight, much like Miller said, once looked at in the context of his actual secret.

So, what could prompt a golfer (who hit that many balls and spent every waking hour for almost half of his life tinkering with his swing to prevent hooking) to make such statements? The answer is simple and straightforward. Hogan found the key that he was looking for and, to his delight, it allowed him to drop nearly all the protective moves that he had worked into his swing over a decade or more, in favor of making his normal swing without fear of hitting his bad shot (the hook). The only thing he did not drop, or more properly that he added, was pronation. It is really that simple. Now how he found this out is a bit more complex and the actual key to the story – the only secret that has not been revealed.

Some of the other questions brought up previously are a bit more complicated, but relatively straightforward, nonetheless. I have given increasingly greater consideration to a number of these questions over the years and have come to believe that I have explanations for quite a few of them. So what is left to be answered? The important matters (in my judgment) to address directly are the following: whether Hogan had a secret or secrets that he did not reveal and the reason why (I contend that he did have secrets and I provide the main reason why he did not reveal them); why he seemingly gave different secrets to different people while according to some, "stringing us along" (I believe he gave different swing tips as "secrets" for specific reasons to specific people and he did not want to adversely affect others whom the tips or secrets would not be applicable or benefit); who Henny Bogan was and where he fits in this story (there is more to come on this); how Hogan came to achieve goodness and then greatness; how I came by the conclusions I reached in the book; and finally, the implication of these revelations for the average golfer. I hope that by the end of these explanations, you might have a Henny Bogan moment or two for yourself, if you are so inclined.

CHAPTER THREE

Manifest Destiny ~ Solving the Puzzle

"I was one of the beginners of it (practice).
The other players used to laugh at me, going out there and practicing after I played, until I started winning; then they joined me."
Ben Hogan

What would it be worth to you if you could cut to the heart of the matter on your chosen path, if you knew exactly what to do to succeed at your life's goal? Imagine the peace of mind and deliberate focus you could bring to bear on the task at hand if you had "it," the key piece or blueprint that would enable you to achieve your goals. I often use the analogy of a "nirvana effect," a *Twilight Zone*-like example to describe this elusive concept, where all the traffic lights are green and there are no delays on Interstate 66, allowing me to get to the Washington Navy Yard in forty-two minutes flat rather than over an hour. (It has never happened; forty-seven minutes on the weekend is my record!) If I could produce the "nirvana effect" on demand, the time savings alone would be like having a twenty-six-hour day. Life is unfortunately not like the *Twilight Zone*, at least not in that respect. You can't count on this type of fortuitous occurrence as a basis of your plans, for instance. But you can certainly be optimistic and hope that it happens. In the final analysis, like most concepts or constructs, it's the type of fanciful thing that you need not do anything deliberate or constructive about, since hope is not a plan! As they say: "Trust in Allah, but tie up your camel!"

But what if in the context of this somewhat fanciful state of affairs we could apply the same logic to a more specific or pragmatic example such as work, or perhaps our golf game? What if you took your golf game to a level of execution where, with one culminating or final tip or one secret, you mastered your swing and actually got over the top and suddenly found "it?" The idea or notion of having "it," the "nirvana effect" wherein you possess the key piece or essential element required to solve a problem, is not some fanciful dream or idealized state of affairs where logic and belief are suspended, as in my traffic example. That is not at all what I am referring to as "it," that is, no lamp, no genie, no three wishes, but instead a pragmatic plan or a blueprint that could be followed with certitude, like the building of a house or a structure. The result should be tangible and repeatable, immutable.

The example I suggested has as its core premise an idealized end-state objective that would make commuting easier. But applied to your life or your goals and desires, it takes on a more pragmatic nature, such as the realization of your dreams, goals, or a lifelong pursuit that remains somewhat abstract because, although you have never dropped everything you were doing in pursuit of it, you have never quite given up on achieving it, either.

From the standpoint of golf, as odd as it may strike you at first hearing, we golfers, be we novices, occasional players or, that rarest among us, "scratch golfers," have much in common with the great Ben Hogan. Long before he won sixty-four tournaments on the professional tour, including nine major championships, and becoming a living legend, renowned as the greatest golf ball striker of all time, Hogan aspired to learn the game of golf and to simply hit the golf ball. Having hit the ball, he strove to repeat that simple action, with an aim to hit it better or more solidly. Building on that success, he sought to refine the swing action that allowed him to hit the golf ball solidly, in order to gain consistency. When that refined swing action produced consistent, solid contact he became more serious about the direction and aim of his golf shots. The refined swing action was easier to repeat, which fostered more consistent and solid contact, producing a more consistent shot flight and trajectory, which allowed him to get somewhat fussier about aiming and the target chosen as the object of the strike.

Hogan became better and better at producing a repeating swing, which translated into a consistency that allowed him to become objective or target-focused to the point where the swing action became second nature. Hogan caught the "golfing fever" somewhere along the development way, which is a somewhat tongue-in-cheek reference to the desire all golfers experience, however fleeting in nature, when the stars and planets align and they manage to hit a shot or two that fosters delusions of grandeur or a taste of perfection and a sense of achievability. Hogan would later put this moment and the nature of "golfing fever" in perspective in his own way and words in his book *Five Lessons*: "One of the greatest pleasures in golf – I can think of nothing that truly compares with it unless it is watching a well-played shot streak for the flag – is the sensation a golfer experiences at the instant he contacts the ball flush, and correctly. He always knows when he does, for then and only then does a distinctive 'sweet feeling' sweep straight up the shaft from the clubhead, and surge through his arms and his whole frame."

New golfers experiencing this elusive, coincidental happy accident of alignment (amidst the cancellation of all manner of swing faults to produce sweet contact like the proverbial lightning in a bottle), have an almost religious sense of wonderment, fulfillment and, well, a sweet feeling! These elusive circumstantial accidents can motivate golfers for entire seasons!

For each of us there is a latent "it" of some type, the connotation of which relates to what you aspire to or what you would most like to do. If you continuously worked at it and somehow developed your own "nirvana effect," or discovered that breakthrough element or technique that put you over the top, would you dedicate much time and effort pursuing the fruition of such a plan? Of course you would. If you walked away from the idea entirely, satisfied to leave it at the conceptual level, what answer could you possibly have for the "man in the glass" every time his accusatory look found you? So let's say you did decide to pursue achieving "it." Perhaps you fell prey to and followed the siren's call, implemented the blueprint, and found that your efforts to master your craft approached your wildest expectations, and you further sensed or believed that you truly had a chance to make your mark on a grand scale. How hard would you work at the newfound end-state objective in pursuit of the fruition of your dreams? And how hard would you work to stay there once you realized the dream? If you were a golfer who thought that hitting a thousand golf balls a day for the next two years might enable you to become a pro golfer, would you do it? Could you do it? Would you risk it? How many would you hit for how long to be the number-one golfer in the world? How about if you thought you could be the greatest golfer of all time? Would you shoulder the burden and take it head-on announcing your intent like Tiger Woods did?

Much of the available literature about Ben Hogan disregards the above direct questions as if they are somehow not operative or in some way not worthy of consideration. In place of these more worthwhile queries, the golfing public these past decades has often been treated to rhetorical variations of the same relatively insignificant and trivial issues, and questioning why Hogan practiced so much. Why did he hit so many golf balls those years from 1932-38 when he truly wasn't very good, with a self-described swing that was "awful?" And once he finally achieved better results in the 1938-42 timeframe and in the post-World War II period, why did he continue to beat golf balls? And once he truly got to the summit, as evidenced by the results achieved in 1946 and subsequent years, why did he continue to hit golf balls as if he still had something to prove or as if he feared he was going to suddenly lose it? After his accident in 1949, he hit golf balls to recover his technique, but he never stopped hitting them until he was physically unable to do so, well beyond the point where he competed anymore, while (baffling to some) shunning opportunities to play on the fledgling senior tour.

Were Hogan an average or somewhat lesser-achieving golfer, the discussion would be largely academic, since his accomplishments would have left him simply an oddity. But the methodology he followed made him a legend in his own lifetime. He was still playing world-class golf at the advanced age of fifty-five, as evidenced by his record back-nine score of thirty and a top ten finish at the 1967 Masters. Hogan's story has largely been told and yet remains clouded or shrouded in mystery and secrets to this day. In light of all the practice and dedication over such a sustained period, is it too difficult to accept that he simply wanted to be the best golfer in the world and he practiced as much as he thought necessary to achieve that end?

And how did he get to be so good? Just from practicing? Or was there more to it than simply digging it out of the dirt? He revealed elements of his swing and his secret over time through articles and columns, including *Power Golf*, *Life* magazine articles, as well as his classic instruction manual *Five Lessons*. Hogan insinuated sometime later that he apparently had some other secret technique that went beyond what he described in the *Life* articles. He offered to sell his secret sometime after these were published, but negotiations broke down.

But if he did have some other secret that he thought might benefit golfers, why did he not reveal it in his lifetime? And how do we explain why so many have tried with so little success to duplicate his efforts using the methodology he outlined? There are other matters to clarify in addition to those touched on previously, as well, such as his apparent predilection for sharing his golfing "secrets" with others, who were then enlisted as co-conspirators who were admonished not to share the techniques. With his passing in 1997 came the inevitable revelations of some of those agreements and the surprising discovery that he told different secrets to different people, each of whom was convinced they were given "the" secret.

These revelations have clarified only the obvious point that there is no apparent single secret technique per se, at least not the type of secret that can be applied like an elixir or bromide to fix what ails us golfers, enabling us to play championship-level golf. The other obvious clarification is that Hogan helped people with their swings throughout his lifetime in what was from all appearances a sincere effort to share his golf knowledge. It seems at least odd, if not inexplicable, why he would deliberately withhold information that he thought would benefit the average golfer. Or similarly, why he gave *different* secrets to different golfers, when they were obviously all people he was sincere about helping improve their golf. Just how many secrets were there in the Hogan closet? Even a cursory scrutiny of these details makes it readily apparent that there are different concepts for what is a "secret." These secrets were to those golfers what Hogan's secrets were to him. Specifically, they were nothing more or less than personal modifications to basic fundamentals in order to accommodate idiosyncrasies, compensations for swing faults as opposed to actual secrets.

Another matter of somewhat lesser importance to some, though no less puzzling, was the infrequent though sustained reports of his habit of using an odd name at times when he was introduced to people. Or his occasional tendency when answering the telephone or signing a letter or note, to refer to himself as "Henny Bogan." Now Hogan was well known as a perfectionist and fussy to a fault about not only all that he did, but also what was done around him and what was done on his behalf. It stretches credulity to think that he simply got his name wrong at times or was making some apparent joke that nobody else seems to have been privy to, notwithstanding the name plate on his desk given to him by his employees identifying him as "Henny Bogan." The little matter of clarifying what is what and so about Hogan's secrets must somehow include an explanation for all manners of detail large and small, including this Henny Bogan character.

    The story of Ben Hogan's trials and tribulations is of interest to anyone who struggles to perfect their technique and to thereby distinguish themselves from their peers. That's what Hogan did in his lifetime. That he was successful is not in dispute; we can probably agree on that point. It is not even remotely controversial that he is a perennial figure on everyone's list of all-time greatest golfers. His tournament results alone refute any notion to the contrary. Many believe he was the best ball striker *ever*, a man who was watched and followed by fans and peers alike, as well as the generations of golfers that followed him, like no golfer before or since. The context here is not the same adulation, however, that Arnold Palmer enjoyed when he provided the inspiration for "Arnie's Army." No one who watched Arnold swing a club ever puzzled for long over what he did or how he achieved his success. He simply overpowered the golf course when he was playing well. But his swing is not an action that is well suited for the average golfer. One could argue that Tiger Woods inspires a similar following; but much like Arnold before him, the inspiration spoken of is not the same as in the Hogan context. Woods shares a similarity to Palmer, of prodigious length and of athletic, skilled application with near daredevil-like shot-making, the likes of which have not been seen before – and more so applicable to Woods, an ability to produce on course shots and deeds that his peers widely acknowledge they are not capable of replicating.

    Hogan's case is different and I think the easiest way to describe the difference without sidetracking the discussion is to state simply that the majority of people were swept up in the emotion of the moment watching Arnold Palmer or Tiger Woods, to see *what* each did; whereas people, including fellow golfers, watched Hogan to see *how* he did it. The difference is significant and meaningful, in a transcendental way. Woods and Palmer's triumphs at Augusta, for instance, have been described at various times as being welcomed by the loudest, most raucous roars imaginable, perhaps the loudest cheers ever heard on that hallowed ground. Whereas Ben Hogan's record-setting back-nine score of thirty in 1967 was reportedly welcomed at each hole by a "reserved standing ovation," consisting of applause that has been described as "like quiet but persistent rain showers." Heavy stuff indeed!

We all face struggles in our daily lives and Hogan's early struggles were no different. That he desired to get better as a professional and that he aspired to be a great golfer, in fact, the greatest ever should be the first point conceded when one attempts to account for why he did what he did, the way he did it. He was committed and determined to get better; and he wanted to be the best! Is there something unclear, problematic, or difficult about explaining or understanding this objective? Available literature still contains references from the modern era that indicate that some still puzzle over this basic fundamental issue. He was not out to save enough for a ranch and retire to it like Byron Nelson, or to make enough to live like a millionaire like Walter Hagen's aspiration, or to have some good results that would allow him to make a good living and be in the top 125 like some modern-day pros. He quite simply wanted to be the greatest golfer of all time.

The question of why he practiced so much is also relatively trivial in comparison to some of the bigger issues that should be answered, but I think it is important to put it into context. Hogan committed to practice early on to become good enough to compete on the tour. He enjoyed it so much that practice became ingrained as a habit, long after it had fulfilled its purpose, and he continued it long after it was necessary. I described him as a belt-and-suspenders guy because he employed overkill in his approach to practice by taking it to a level where he knew no one could possibly follow. He liked to practice and was committed to getting better at golf; there was no other way for him to accomplish it (in his mind) than to practice, practice, and practice. So the "optimism and construction" or first stage of his career saw him practicing every waking hour from 1932 through 1937 to integrate the proper techniques into his swing and to solidify his fundamentals, including the proper leg action, hip turn, and the waggle. He was given advice and tips at various times during his development, including the observation that he tended to regrip the club at the top of his swing. He also worked to perfect his golf course management or strategy skills.

Hogan considered practice as the price of admission or the down payment that enabled him to compete with the other pros. He was in pursuit of his vision whereby he was going to have total mastery over the golf ball and he apparently remained convinced throughout this timeframe that it was within reach. When he weakened his grip in the defensive or second stage of his career in 1938 and discovered the importance of the swing plane, he was reinvigorated from the standpoint of perfecting his golf swing. He worked to ingrain the new fundamentals in his swing. Often lost in this discussion is the context of when and how he made these changes. It is important to maintain the reference that Hogan made the swing changes in the midst of the golf season while playing in tournaments, which he depended upon to support his wife Valerie and himself. Hogan did not have the luxury of taking time off to ingrain the new techniques, so he somehow found a way to balance the integration effort while not suffering any marked drop in the quality or level of his tournament play.

Though fellow pros thought Hogan was crazy to hit so many golf balls, there was a method to his madness. He was using those practice sessions to integrate and refine his technique. He had the discipline and the drive, as well as the motivation, to somehow separate his practice efforts and his work on his emerging skills from the day-to-day skills necessary to compete and make money on the tour. From 1938 through the War up to early 1946, he practiced to integrate the new elements in the defensive stage, intended to obviate or abate, while not quite eliminating, his problematic hook through swing techniques, but not change his fundamentals per se. I attribute this choice of approach on Hogan's part to a concern over any loss of distance that would have necessarily accompanied more fundamental swing changes. There is a tendency by some to speculate or dwell on the wrong aspects of Hogan's motivations in a manner that treats his efforts as unusual or his methodology as somewhat dogmatic. But considered in light of the major swing changes accomplished by recent champions, for instance, the changes undertaken by Nick Faldo and Tiger Woods, Hogan can more charitably be viewed as ahead of his time. The breakthrough (stage three) period of his career began after the Masters, April–May 1946, when he discovered the technique that allowed him to solve his hooking problem once and for all, while retaining his distance and also resolving his low ball flight issues. His practice from that point forward ingrained the discovered technique, but was more along the lines of normal practice – shot-making, rather than his previous efforts of the past decade-and-a-half where he focused on all manner of anti-hook techniques.

This was evident in his statement about how he came to realize that he "no longer had to try to do a bunch of little things perfectly..." That does not mean he was done practicing and, make no mistake about it, he was still competing on tour, and he still needed the time to integrate the new technique within his swing, his strategy, and his risk calculus. So there was much to practice. For instance, could the technique be used out of the sand? Did weather, moisture, or heavy rough affect the technique?

After the 2 February 1949 accident, he entered the optimism and reclamation (stage four) part of his career where he had to practice to regain his strength, technique, skill, and game. The proof that he had resolved his problems once and for all were immediately demonstrated by the phenomenal speed of his recovery. Having successfully recovered his health and his game, the vindication or fulfillment (stage five) period of his career was when he sustained his regained ability through consistent practice, but somewhat sporadic play. It is doubtful he could have played championship-level golf without consistent practice at this stage of his career. His body had changed dramatically from a flexibility, stamina, and strength standpoint. The constant practice must have been very difficult and hard on his ravaged body. But as evidenced by his results in the 1960 U.S. Open Championship and his top ten finish in the 1967 Masters, he was still capable of championship golf in his later years and well into his fifties.

The answer as to why he practiced so much over a sustained period of time is as relatively simple as the above explanation indicates. He practiced to get to the point where he was good enough to compete; he continued practicing to get better, seeking to perfect his swing and work through his hook problems while he was competing; he practiced to integrate the breakthrough techniques he discovered; he practiced to regain his game and his health; and finally, he practiced because he loved it!

CHAPTER FOUR

Why Did Hogan Not Reveal His Secret?

"I held Hogan in great respect and, to some degree, some awe."
Arnold Palmer

"I don't get in awe of many people, but just to be able
to say I met him was something. The meeting meant a lot to me
because there are only a couple of golfers you can put up there on a pedestal,
Jack Nicklaus being one and Ben Hogan the other."
Greg Norman

"Tiger Woods' record may someday mark him as the
greatest player of all time, but the greatest ball striker?
No, no that would certainly be Ben Hogan by a wide margin."
Jack Nicklaus

"Anyone can say they have a secret if they don't tell what it is!"
Sam Snead

There are few topics in sports that elicit a more immediate reaction than that of Ben Hogan and his famous secret, at least among golfers. There is no apparent middle ground in this debate, perhaps reflecting the increasingly vitriolic nature of the tone of national debate on all things large and small. The time for closure on this matter is clearly long overdue and is just as clearly not satisfied. Why did this honorable man, who otherwise disclosed everything he knew about the golf swing via his two seminal works on the topic, including his classic book *Five Lessons*, seemingly string people along by not making a definitive statement during his lifetime?

The point obviously is made in consideration of the assumption that: (1) one believes there are secrets; (2) the secrets have not been revealed; and (3) there is a credible rationale explaining why not. I think the "why he did not disclose" question is an important point to establish before we attend to the business of the secret itself. Myriad evidence exists for those seeking a reason why he did not disclose the information in his lifetime, but that evidence is only obvious in hindsight. The truth of the matter is that Hogan revealed through his instruction books everything he felt was necessary for golfers to learn the game. He explained his secret (pronation) in *Life* magazine and he put the secret in the proper context of the fundamentals he advocated by omitting it from *Five Lessons*.

Hogan's approach to explaining the rationale and facts surrounding why he choose to do something a certain way was repeated throughout his life so often that it can be used as a descriptive term, as in the context of a "Hoganesque or Hogan-like" response. Hogan had a "Garbo-like" reputation in that regard. He was downright stingy with explanations most of the time but he was far more likely not to address issues at all. Throughout his career mini-controversies raged around Hogan, fueled by a complex combination of those who were not particularly enamored by his less-than-cooperative nature, his own inattention, and the desire by some to increase circulation. He was a 20 handicap when it came to public relations and was often caught off guard; he never took the initiative to attempt to head issues off early through full disclosure. As a result, his uneasy relationship with most print media and sports journalists bordered on hostile or adversarial and was always on the brink of bursting into flame.

This uneasy relationship with the media mellowed and improved somewhat after his accident in 1949 but was rekindled anew in the mid-to-late 1950s as Arnold Palmer grew in favor and people naturally gravitated to his "Army." We often forget as a matter of convenience how hateful fans can be to the other team or the other guy in the context of sports. But Hogan felt some of the ire and wrath that Jack Nicklaus later experienced in spades and Gary Player to a lesser, but more intense degree, as those two talented golfers came to the fore as great golfers. In the rights of succession that is a golf tradition as old as the sport, Hogan inherited the mantle of the best golfer almost by default when Byron Nelson retired in 1946; though, as I mentioned earlier it was almost grudgingly accorded to Hogan because there were some inclined to refer to Nelson as the best long after his retirement. This was somewhat in keeping with the confusion caused by the contrast of amateur and professional golf that lingered somewhat up to the ascension of Palmer. When Bobby Jones retired from golf as an amateur and the consensus best player, it was years before there was agreement on who the best golfer was because people made a distinction between the pros and amateurs. Gene Sarazen replaced Walter Hagen in the professional ranks up to the early 1930s, but Jones' reputation as the greatest lingered long after his retirement, despite his largely ceremonial play. Hogan's affirmation was confirmed through his stellar results starting in 1946 and lasted through 1956. Palmer's wrenching of the title from Hogan over time occurred against the backdrop of the final throes of the death of the amateur as claimant to the throne, well chronicled in *The Match*.

Hogan ended his competitive career and began largely ceremonial play in somewhat of the same uneasy relationship with the media that typified his years of play. A small loyal band of Hogan supporters wrote mostly favorable press, but the bulk of the press corps took up support of the new "king" and there was no room for the deposed. For those writers who covered the golf beat and spanned the generations, there were old scars and scores to settle, as anyone who had ever suffered the sting of an icy Hogan glare or the bite of an acidic, "I do not suffer fools lightly" rebuke, could attest.

Hogan did not help matters with his somewhat strained relationship with Palmer that sparked a series of mini-storms right up through the late 1960s. Hogan was not impressed with Palmer's go-for-broke style and felt he survived with his putter. Palmer was a bit aggravated that Hogan never referred to him by name. Hogan liked Ken Venturi quite a bit and was no doubt a supporter of Venturi's point that Palmer had received favorable treatment over a controversial drop at the 1958 Masters. When Hogan was the 1967 Ryder Cup Captain, he and Palmer jousted throughout the matches. Palmer arrived late in his aircraft and "buzzed" the golf course before landing, causing Hogan to welcome him with words to the effect that he had not yet made the team. Hogan sat Palmer down for one of the afternoon matches. If Hogan were not by the mid-1950s already gun-shy and reticent to open up a proverbial flank to those itching to fling some mud and vitriol his way, then he certainly became that way as Palmer predominated into the next decade.

Hogan was simply a man of few words who believed in letting his clubs do his talking. He often stated that people don't seem to appreciate modesty and he likely had a deep memory of those who belittled his practice regimes and methodology in the early days and paid scant attention to his progress. Hogan's silence and grudging participation in the publicity side of the tour was an established practice for several decades, exacerbated by a number of unfortunate incidents over the years that had spiraled into bad press through a combination of loosely reported facts and Hogan's silence.

These incidents are detailed in many other books and each unfolded in the same way, with an initial story that included a range of truth, fiction, and distortion. Hogan rarely commented on extraneous details that in his mind were unrelated to golf, resulting in perpetuation and expansion as the story was spread by the newswire or newspaper services, with embellishment added along the way. If the story did not fade away immediately, it was almost always too late to reverse the adverse perceptions about Hogan by the time he deemed it a necessity to weigh-in. The list of these incidents is long indeed, involving such things as groove sharpening allegations on multiple occasions, Ryder Cup "gerrymandering-like" accusations and a beef scandal, premature retirement stories, appearance money controversies, leaving a tournament he thought he'd lost early only to discover that the leader collapsed making Hogan the winner in absentia, etc.

One of the earliest imbroglios involved Hogan and Nelson's playoff for the 1940 Texas Open played at Brackenridge Park, San Antonio. Tied for first place and heading for a playoff the next day, they were interviewed by a local radio station looking to provide publicity and to drum up some interest. Nelson's portion of the interview went fine and he said some innocuous, respectful things. Hogan stunned the affable Nelson when he said, "Byron's got a good game but it'd be a lot better if he'd practice. Byron is too lazy to practice." Hogan's thoughtless statement stung and whether intended as a bit of a joke or a jab of some type, his relationship with Byron was likely strained from that point forward. Byron won the playoff in a display of golf that indicated he practiced "enough."

Hogan was not on tour to be liked, and nothing about the manner in which he conducted himself said differently or was affected by the non-golf side of the business. Hogan essentially missed the opportunity to disclose the methodology by which he discovered the importance of pronation to his golf swing when the *Life* article was published in 1955. His reticence to revisit the issue of how he solved his swing problems and risk subjecting himself to ridicule was the greatest impediment, thereafter, to disclosure – not lack of or proper financial incentive, not misplaced belief or self-delusion of retaining options for a potential golf comeback, not a desire to trifle with or mess with people, or to continue to mystify for no reason. I believe he decided against disclosure as much out of concern for his wife's protection as for his own piece of mind and that of his family. No longer able to let his clubs do his talking for him, he had no intention of spending the remainder of his life explaining and re-explaining all the details that were largely irrelevant (from his standpoint).

Hogan was continually sought out by fans and players alike throughout his retirement years and there was an instance of a person stalking the Hogans toward the latter stages of his life, resulting in the startled Hogan driving through his garage door in his haste to shake him. Hogan was a public figure who spanned the great information divide between print and broadcast media, as well as the emergence of the digital age and the Internet. He was much more accessible, and therefore vulnerable, than any average golfer of the modern era.

Curt Sampson's book *Hogan* is a case in point for illustrating my belief that Ben Hogan took his secret to the grave for fear of further mischaracterization, endless speculation, and ridicule. Sampson's uncharitable approach to the Hogan story struck me as mean-spirited and dogmatic, particularly in the manner in which the author described Hogan's relationships and supposed lack of friends. Sampson took the book in a direction that attempted to link Hogan's "obsessive" love for golf with his father's suicide – a topic Hogan avoided discussing throughout his adult life. A characteristic of most pro golfers is their love for the game and most pursue its mastery without ever having their motivations questioned or their actions "diagnosed." Many also have tragic events associated with their lives, however, few find it necessary to link or describe their motivation to play in terms of these events. These days it is accepted as a norm that pro golfers need to be a bit selfishly focused and obsessive about their fitness and golf routines to maintain their skills. Hogan was way ahead of his time from that standpoint. Sampson also adopted a disingenuous familiarity throughout by referring to Hogan as "Bennie." Out of respect for Hogan's mastery, even later-generation golf professionals continue to refer to him as "Mr. Hogan."

That some of Hogan's peers and friends referred to him as "Benny" or "Bennie" is part of the humanity of the game, the chumminess attributable to the barnstorming-like nature of the post-depression pro tour. In a video clip showing Sam Snead and Ben Hogan greeting each other and conversing in adjoining fairways at the 1967 Masters, they can be seen chiding each other about their "paunches." Imagine the stories those two old bulls must have swapped over the years regarding their rivalry!

The bottom line is: I believe that Hogan did not reveal the manner in which he discovered his secret simply because he was not interested in providing fodder for any cheap-shot artists who might be prone to describe his technique in the worst possible light. Period.

The words of President Theodore Roosevelt come to mind: "There is no more unhealthy being, no man less worthy of respect, than he who either really holds, or feigns to hold, an attitude of sneering disbelief toward all that is great and lofty, whether in achievement or in that noble effort which, even if it fails, comes to second achievement. A cynical habit of thought and speech, a readiness to criticize work which the critic himself never tries to perform, an intellectual aloofness which will not accept contact with life's realities – all these are marks, not as the possessor would feign to think, of superiority, but of weakness. They mark the men unfit to bear their part painfully in the stern strife of living, who seek, in the affection of contempt for the achievements of others, to hide from others and from themselves in their own weakness."

CHAPTER FIVE

Practice, Practice, Practice; Trials and Tribulations Lead to a Precipice

"Some things you try don't work out,
so you just go back and find something that does work."
Ben Hogan

When Hogan was asked throughout his career to explain why he practiced so much, he always responded the same way; he had to because his swing was lousy. He could just as easily have said it was because he wanted to be the best player in the world and the only way he felt like he was trying to the utmost degree and could be at peace with himself was to make use of every available hour to improve his technique. Regardless, his explanation has often been dismissed by many out of hand in favor of fanciful psychological theories or categorized as an insufficient or unsatisfactory response.

Golf seems to bring out the critic in all of us. We rarely question the powerful motivations that drive top athletes in most other sports or other endeavors, such as music or the Olympics. If an amateur collegian and hopeful Olympic swimmer dedicated his or her life to practice and set a goal to win every race, would anyone question that athlete's practice habits (unless they were unsuccessful)? We typically judge athletes and sports by results, and there can be no such lingering concerns in hindsight regarding Hogan's capability of achieving the goals he set for himself. The earliest statement of his goal (to be the greatest golfer of all time) was reportedly around the age of thirteen in response to a question from his mother as to why he did not take a regular job like his older brother. Hogan clearly achieved what he set out to achieve via the methodology and course that he pursued. Could Hogan have done just as well with less work and effort and practice? If it did not matter to him, why does it matter to us, unless we hope to emulate his success?

Hogan changed the game forever with his dogmatic approach to practice, solidifying its place as one of the elements to be addressed on the path to greatness. Players routinely hit the range after their rounds today, and that is somewhat a measure of who among them is serious about their golf. But Hogan was singularly focused on golf success, with no impediments or distractions to that pursuit until later in his career, when his golf-club-making business required some measure of attention.

His dedication and the large amount of time he spent practicing was a sharp contrast to those of his era and those who immediately followed. The opposite of his approach was Jack Nicklaus, who hit enough balls to get in shape for the season and then enough to maintain it. Unless he was working on something specific, he did not bang golf balls for the sake of practice. In contrast to Hogan, Nicklaus had many outside pursuits, the most important of which was raising his family. That he could balance a large family and achieve such a remarkable record is quite a tribute to his time-management skills (and it says a lot about his wife Barbara's support).

At the opposite extreme from Hogan is pro golfer Bruce Lietzke. His caddy found it difficult to believe that a top-flight golfer could go the entire off season without touching a club. He put a banana in one of his head covers at the end of the season and discovered to his chagrin that it was still there the next season at the first tournament stop!

Regarding Hogan, it is ironic that over the years this same skepticism about why he practiced and the need for so much practice was often followed shortly thereafter by curiosity or speculation as to how Hogan became so good. How he went from a self-professed lousy golf swing, and a game that was not competitive on the pro tour through 1937, to the top of the game in the ensuing years, becoming the leading money winner three years in a row, and a consistent top-five finisher in the years that followed. Is it possible to outwork everyone to get to the top of the golf world? Would that be so unusual, given other sports where athletes, in essence, do the same thing?

Given myriad possibilities to characterize Hogan's story, I think a convenient way to look at it is in the groupings or stages that I have described over time, structured along the course of his life. I described five stages at the macro level, largely defined by his struggles and successes throughout the germane periods. These are snapshots of a sort that tell where he was at "in the movie" at a given point in time. I will lightly touch on the period leading up to the breakthrough in 1946 and discuss thereafter the implications.

One issue that stands out quite a bit when you approach his story this way is how little time Hogan had available to him once he found his game. Less than three years elapsed from the time of his breakthrough in the spring of 1946 until his accident in 1949. As a well-known oldie's song relates, Hogan did not have much time left in "his bottle" to do the things he wanted to do once he found them.

The periods of interest are:
- 1912-32, from his birth until he joined the pro tour at nineteen;
- 1932-37, the so-called formative years including the first three times he went broke and had to leave the tour, leading up to the time just before he started to achieve success;
- 1938 to early 1946, including his first period of success that was interrupted by his service in World War II, and leading up to when he hit the wall after the Masters Tournament;
- 1946-49, the period wherein he found his game, won the inaugaural Colonial Invitational, achieved the successes he had aspired to, and was then cut short by the accident;
- 1949-50, the recovery period;
- 1950-60, vindication and phenomenal success on a much-reduced competitive schedule, and the end of his phenomenal run at competitive golf; and finally,
- 1960-97, when he further reduced his play until his death.

Long before Hogan's secret became "the secret," there were the trials, tribulations, and travails of the formative period of his career from turning pro at seventeen until early 1938, when he first started to achieve the success that spelled survival along his chosen path. He was hardly ready to become a pro golfer at age seventeen, but that was the limit age-wise for the Glen Garden Caddy Yard and Hogan did not aspire to school or some other option that came with an opportunity to practice and play golf. He was forced to compete long before he was mentally or physically ready (skills-wise), so it is not a complete surprise that he went broke several times over these years, returning to Ft. Worth to work on his game and save money for another attempt. He literally built his competitive game from the ground up during this period, integrating many of the pieces of his swing that came to define his distinctive action. He came by most of them by playing with and watching his fellow pros, and by making use of that sincerest form of flattery, imitation. Hogan's friends called him "Bennie" during this period, but his nickname later was "The Hawk," because he rarely missed anything that passed before his eyes. An oddity that was observed by self-professed Hogan disciple John Shlee in his excellent instruction manual *Maximum Golf*, was that, of all the top pros photographed striking a golf ball, each had his eyes shut at the moment of impact but one. Hogan had his eyes wide open.

Hogan kept his eyes wide open from an early age. He outlines in *Five Lessons* how he came to learn some of the fundamentals associated with a sound swing and how he incorporated these elements into his own swing. He cites age thirteen as when he made his first really important swing change, attributable to caddying for and watching an amateur player named Ed Stewart at Glen Garden Club in Fort Worth. Hogan adjusted the action of his left knee based on observations of Stewart's swing. Early in his days on tour in 1932 he incorporated into his game the waggle action of renowned short-game specialist Johnny Revolta.

Revolta employed a different waggle based on the type of shot he was playing (whether feathery pitch, choppy bump and run, or delicate bunker shot) as part of his pre-shot routine. Hogan integrated the technique into his routine for all his shots. Lest we think Hogan was unique in this regard (e.g., mimicry), his good friend and Florida practice-round companion Claude Harmon later arranged for Revolta to play a round with him and his sons, all destined to be instructors, in order for them to be similarly exposed to the technique of this short-game genius

(as reported by Claude "Butch" Harmon Jr. in his book *The Pro*.)

At some point early on, perhaps in 1937, Harry "Light Horse" Cooper gave Hogan some advice about his tendency to regrip the club on his backswing, a fault Sam Snead later described as "playing the flute" on the backswing. Hogan also described how he solidified and incorporated the image of the proper hip turn in the mid-thirties by watching movie reels of the top golfers of the day, including Hagen, Sarazen, and Jones, although most likely attributable to movie reels of Bobby Jones.

Tom Watson refers to a Wild Bill Melhorn drill in his book *Getting Back to Basics,* performed by placing a club across his thighs and turning around it as a way to work on making the knees and lower body more flexible, active, and involved in the swing. Hogan played quite a bit of golf with Mehlorn, who was known to be a keen student of the game at a time when it was not necessarily considered important or even an element of playing better golf. His influence regarding "swinging well below yourself" is evident in the swing sequence tip Hogan provides on the trailer of the Shell's Wonderful World of Golf match where he plays Sam Snead at the Houston Country Club, Houston, Texas, (aired February 21 1965). As an aside, Hogan won this showdown of the titans, hitting every fairway and green, while putting on an absolute clinic during the match. Snead was no slouch either, having a tough day with the putter but striking the ball beautifully. The notion of starting the forward swing with the knees and the lower body moving well beneath you is the focus of Mehlorn's drill and Hogan's tip.

Hogan's play in the Oakland Open in January, 1938, formed the basis for what later became known as his icy, isolated on-course demeanor. He was down to his last eighty-six dollars and he and Valerie were surviving on hamburgers and oranges to save money to get from event to event. When he came out in the morning to go to the golf course for the final round he found his car on blocks (or rocks) and his tires gone. Having his tires stolen at such a desperate time no doubt fueled an anger that caused him to bear down like never before with the urgency of life and death. He was literally playing for his golfing life and the $286 he won for sixth place signaled the end of their struggles (in hindsight). He later referred to Oakland as the biggest check he would ever see in terms of importance to his career. He cited 1938 as the year he finally grasped the concept of the swing plane, after struggling for some years with a faulty concept of how his backswing should flow.

Seven decades later, Claude "Butch" Harmon, Jr. described in *The Pro*, how important this Hogan fundamental element of the swing plane was to Tiger Woods. Much like Hogan before him, Tiger is swinging at speeds most humans and cars are not capable of achieving. Harmon's explanation of the ramifications of a faulty or inconsistent swing plane cites Hogan's "pane of glass" concept, as well as his personal experiences playing with Hogan and his father, Masters Champion and legendary Club Pro Claude Harmon. Further, for Hogan, at five feet, eight inches and 140 pounds in his prime, to hit the ball the length he was capable of with the equipment and the golf balls of his day, was nothing short of miraculous. He was clearly generating "Tiger-like" swing speed numbers himself.

This was also the same timeframe in which Henry Picard helped Hogan make a grip adjustment that brought his hands well on top of the club as a way to preclude or prevent his problematic and unpredictable hook. His practice regimen was already an oddity among fellow pro golfers, often consisting of multiple sessions of several hundred balls per session hitting every club in the bag. He also continued practicing late at night in his hotel room, working on memorizing the correct slot or position of the club on his backswing given his swing plane and also working on his chipping and putting. These sessions were dedicated to solidifying and ingraining within his swing these newfound elements.

The initial success he achieved after previously going broke three times and almost going broke again in 1938 appears to have been fostered by at least four important elements: (1) fixes to his grip, including Harry Cooper's advice and Henry Picard's adjustment of his grip position, which at the very least significantly diminished while not eliminating his hooking problems; (2) the solidification of his sense of the fundamentals, including the proper hip movement and that most important element, the concept of the swing plane; (3) increasing self-confidence and reduced self-doubt caused by some perceived assurances of help offered by Henry Picard, and the start of a period where Hogan consistently finished in the money; and (4) landing a club pro job on the recommendation of Henry Picard that paid a wage Hogan could depend upon as a backstop to his golf. He was also signed by Tony Penna to represent MacGregor golf, which paid a paltry, but contributing amount to fund the household. Additionally, he finally broke through and won something – the 1938 Hershey Four Ball with Victor Ghezzi, an invitation that was no doubt extended as a result of a good word by the hosting pro, Picard. Hogan later dedicated *Power Golf* to Henry Picard, which some found somewhat puzzling, but these gestures came at a time when Hogan was struggling and they meant the world to him.

An important element to note that is conspicuously absent from the list of items responsible for contributing to his growing self-confidence was his incorporation of course-management rules to guide his play. Whether fueled by the notion that he played well when angry, based on his Oakland experience or as a direct result of his recognition that he just could not trifle with certain pin positions, this is arguably the most important aspect he integrated in his game during the 1938-46 timeframe. This remained the case for quite some time in light of his inability to completely cure his hook or to hit a fade on demand.

Golf books in general touch on course management all too briefly, but it is just as important an aspect in shooting good golf scores (and just as boring) as field position and clock management are to winning drives in football, or shot selection and position are to billiards, or choice of variations are to dictating chess style. Hogan was later quoted as saying words to the effect that good and consistent results were achievable through average ball-striking combined with good course-management techniques; and that technique accounted for twenty to thirty percent of the important elements to scoring, while course management was seventy to eighty percent.

Tom Watson has an excellent book on the subject called *Tom Watson's Strategic Golf*. While he was not the first to mention the importance of course management, Watson is one of the few to dedicate an entire book to it that does not double as a swing-instruction book. All golfers could benefit from his recommendations to view and play the course as the golf architect designed it, and to figure out why the bunkers are where they are, for instance. I also like his advice to discern the break of greens by figuring out how the architect solved the problem of drainage, easily done in many cases by visualizing how a huge bucket of water dumped on the green would flow away from the pin.

The modern golf-game focus on "air play" notwithstanding (playing courses the "air mail" route by blowing shots over all the trouble), Hogan gained in confidence with deliberate, positive actions as he worked his way around the golf course. The increased self-confidence (or diminished self-doubt) grew over time and exhibited itself as improved results and tournament success. These successes were interrupted during World War II and resumed after Hogan left the service.

He stated in *Five Lessons*, "As I learned more and more about the golf swing and how to play golf, I enjoyed increasing success on the pro circuit." He added, "I was never genuinely confident about my game until 1946. Up to that time, I was never sure before the round whether I would be 69 or 79, and I felt I had no assurances that if I was off my top form that I would be able to post a decent score. While my friends on tour told me not to worry, that I had a grooved swing, my self-doubting never stopped, and I was worried about the next day, and the day after, etc." He describes a sudden change in attitude in 1946, attributable to changing his golf approach from an endless focus on doing a great many difficult things perfectly, to focusing on executing the fundamentals properly. He suddenly realized that his previous efforts to achieve near perfection were neither advisable nor possible nor, more importantly, even necessary. His newfound attitude was based on the belief that the fundamental elements of the swing could be executed well regardless of whether you were sharp that morning, or not. All you needed to do was groove the fundamental movements, and there weren't that many of them. All golfers can empathize with the sentiment of apprehension before play begins and worry about the next day; but most of us spend much more time worrying before the round about what is to come, and during the round on the next shot!

There is nothing new in this shortened version of the story in *Five Lessons*, but there are a few elements about fundamentals that should be explored before we go further. Every pro has above-average fundamentals to begin with, so the notion that a focus on the fundamentals was enough to put someone over the top was a tough sell for those who paid attention to such pronouncements. Much like Hogan before them, there were folks paying utmost attention to his success on tour, as they would to anyone who separated from the pack. Hogan addressed this issue directly in *Five Lessons*. He referred to the questioning of how far one could go with a focus on improving the basic fundamentals as a form of "polite skepticism," expressed as the notion that this focus could somehow be at the center of his newfound consistency. He proffered as just not accurate the rhetoric example of people referring to his recommendations as "about as useful as a pole-vaulter giving the relatively benign advice that once you run, plant the pole, and spring forward, you simply release over the bar." Similarly, the more topical rebuttal couched his example of mastering the golf swing as probably useful "if you had eaten your lunch on the practice tee your whole life," but not applicable to average golfers.

While he acknowledged these points, he dismissed them as not an accurate characterization of the true state of affairs. Hogan truly felt the average golfer of average athletic ability was capable of hitting good shots and breaking 80. The problem and main argument against his premise was that many golfers who employed his methodology did not find the expected immediate success. The theory of the application of the basic fundamentals as a way to improve your golf did not stand up in practice. Golfers were perhaps a bit unrealistic, but they expected more in the way of a demonstrative improvement in their games.

That *Five Lessons* did not reference the *Life* magazine 1955 "secret" article caused some to question what appeared to be a significant and glaring omission. Also missing in his account was another aspect of critical importance and the actual precursor to the events that led to this newfound confidence. The sequence of events leading to the "realization" or breakthrough he describes in 1946 was precipitated by his experiencing anew the same old hooking bugaboo that plagued him early in his career. The problem surfaced infrequently in 1941 and 1942, and then with increasing frequency in 1945-46.

Whether attributable to an onset of the reported back problems he experienced during this time, or caused by a renewed interest in regaining some of his compromised distance resulting from his weak grip, is not particularly clear. He changed his grip when he came out of the service in 1945, adopting the so-called "short thumb" position. He moved his left thumb up the shaft a relatively large amount, which was a fairly significant modification employed to control his loose swing by cutting down on the length of his backswing. This reduced "looseness" by giving him much better control over his backswing, but at the expense of distance. My speculation is that the increasing head-to-head confrontations with Sam Snead and the exposure to his effortless power were forcing Hogan out of the relative safe bounds of his by-now-familiar weakened grip. Hogan knew how to add power and length to his game; he also knew the price of admission.

The problems came to a head with several disappointing showings, as mentioned previously with his twelve top-three finishes in 1945, and his less-than-satisfactory run at the Masters in April 1946, when he three-putted from inside ten feet on the final hole. He was throwing a shot or two away every round with his hooking, and he was having difficulty getting the ball up in the air, even with his trusty four-wood. He took time off from the tour shortly thereafter to determine what to do about it. Accounts vary as to whether he took off two weeks or more and whether he actually went two or four days without touching a golf club while he thought through a solution. I'm not sure how important that detail is and, in the grand scheme of things, it does not really matter. Suffice it to say that whatever time he took off to think about the problem, it was an eternity for someone who hit millions of balls over the years and was accustomed to hitting the equivalent of more than six hundred golf balls a day.

Hogan obviously faced this predicament several times before when he went broke on the tour and was forced into self-examination to find a way to improve his golf. This was somewhat different, as he had already tasted a measure of success both pre-and postwar, but it was similar from the standpoint that he still aspired to greatness; he had the same drive operative that had fueled him in the first place. As mentioned above, conjecture of that earlier time suggests that coupled with the weakened grip adjustment Henry Picard offered, Hogan himself implemented a rigorous course-management regime to ensure that he was able to compete with his newfound grip. The grip was a relatively uncomfortable compromise and admittedly a poor substitute for his long sought-after sound swing that gave him the type of control he desired. But he continued all the while working and practicing to find a better technique. After all, the changes came in the midst of the golf season and he had to make a living. Coupled with solidification of the concept of the swing plane, he laid the cornerstone and subsequently the foundation of his course-management strategy, augmenting his already famous ability to concentrate on the course. These fundamentals were probably born, integrated within his swing, and honed to a razor-sharp edge during this period (1938-46). But he had ridden these changes as far as they could go and he now needed to change the "proverbial horse" and address the problem anew.

CHAPTER SIX

Another Smack at the Wall

"I hate a hook. It nauseates me. I could vomit when I see one.
It's like a rattlesnake in your pocket."
Ben Hogan

Resolving his hooking problem had been deferred as long as humanly possible from the previous timeframe, given Hogan's post-1938 success and the interruption of the war. Hogan was absolutely desperate, driven to do something different this time, motivated by a tremendous desire to pull out all stops to fix his hooking problem. He was a belt-and-suspenders guy, so the fix was something he was going to pursue with desperate over-thoroughness. At risk was the issue of competing in and winning major championships; he could not stand the thought of frittering away another year's worth of opportunities to win the championships that meant the most to him, and continued to elude him.

Each of the previous times he had gone broke and retreated to the practice field, he emerged more motivated and sharper than before; but each attempt had eventually ended in the same unsatisfactory way. The fact that the fixes he adopted in 1938 were no longer of use to him by 1945 could not have been more clear to him, and it was becoming clear to others. He scuttled by his own admission a number of tournaments during these years, attributable mainly to his recurring hooking problems that cost him a shot or several shots a round, depending on the golf course.

The other more deleterious effect of the problem was his inability to be aggressive on holes that did not fit his shot shape. This forced him to either defer aggressive play or, in the cases where he was chasing a leader late in a round, to adopt a strategy on holes where he had no suitable shots in his arsenal to play without choosing a high-risk course of action that ran counter to his course-management mandates. The need to actually reach a solution once and for all, vice a quick fix, motivated him to think about the problem differently and consider his alternatives.

We don't have insight other than his brief accounts during this time period, but he had obviously given long and thoughtful consideration to the issue. I believe he exposed us to his thought processes a decade later in *Five Lessons* with his summary of the eight fundamental steps that a golfer must do to be correct at impact. Hogan unwinds those steps to link them together in a manner that allows them to build one upon the next and establish the boundary conditions necessary to properly get to, and therefore execute, the next step. The resulting chain action and reaction is the summary of the relatively few but critically important true fundamentals of the swing, the mastery of which he convincingly stated would result in shooting scores below 80.

This material is presented in sharp contrast to *Power Golf,* which preceded it, evidence of how Hogan had mastered the integration of the underlying information in the years between 1938 and 1946. The difference is the focus on the essential elements necessary to make a fundamentally sound golf swing presented in a way that fosters complete integration. *Five Lessons* is "master class" level material and it demonstrates precisely what Hogan said all along. In 1938 he knew all the elements required to make a sound swing, but it was less well integrated than it later became in 1946. *Five Lessons* is the proof of that statement.

The time Hogan spent *not* hitting balls during that 1946 furlough may have been spent inventorying every facet of the fundamentals he had worked out to that point. There were a lot of items in the inventory, including the basic fundamentals of a sound swing, the defensive techniques he established over the years to prevent hooking, as well as all the potential alternatives that had been tried and discarded during those years of trying to prevent hitting a hook. This effort could have provided the bulk of the refined material that later went into

Five Lessons.

The detail in *Five Lessons* provides ample proof of Hogan's deep understanding and grasp of the fundamentals of a sound golf swing. Few have disputed the elements he touts therein. Those who take issue with specific aspects often cite differences that appear to be motivated by the need to support their own philosophical recommendations. By and large golfers took issue with the notion that these fundamental elements alone were sufficient to achieve top-flight play, although Hogan was consistent and adamant about touting them for those golfers with a desire to break 80. Regardless, there was a lack of consensus on this point (that fundamentals alone were sufficient to achieve good results) and no lack of opinions regarding the fundamentals themselves. You could say the fundamentals were not as "fundamental" as appears and the following examples amplify this point.

There is probably no better discussion topic to highlight these differences between techniques than that seemingly cut-and-dry aspect of the swing (a blinding flash of the obvious or BFO), the grip. This is the most common issue that confuses beginners and yet it is the most common discussion point in any golf fundamentals book. Hogan provides an indication of the importance he places on this aspect as he dedicates eighteen pages of the main portion of the book to the grip. He discusses other grips, but recommends the Vardon overlapping method as the best. Hogan discusses differences in his implementation, for instance, with the left hand predominately a palm-and-fingers grip. The grip pressure comes from the last three fingers pushing up to hold the club against the palm pad; the right hand is described as a fingers grip, with the pressure coming from the second and third fingers. The "Vs" are formed by the union of the overlapping of the hands pointing to the right eye and the chin, respectively, for the left and right hands. Hogan modifies the grip slightly with the manner in which he overlaps his pinky, but we will leave that point alone.

Many instructors regard this grip as too weak or too neutral for the average golfer. It is believed to create additional problems by making it more difficult to properly cock or release the wrist cock, while also complicating release, thereby inducing a slice in beginning golfers. However, most beginning golfers slice very well already (thank you very much). Many instructors advocate variations of the Vardon grip, with the club more in the fingers of both hands, with a relatively stronger hand position, with the hands rotated to the right or clockwise on the grip. This more classic grip has the "Vs" pointing toward the right ear or shoulder. Other books advocate a much stronger version of the Vardon grip, rotated even further to the right to fight the tendency to slice, while some books advocate augmenting the Vardon by using the interlocking grip – a methodology used by Jack Nicklaus (because of his relatively small hands) and Tiger Woods. There are some golfers who use and advocate the ten-finger grip in which the fingers are all on the club, in fact, many instructors opine that the ten-finger grip is the grip of the future.

I like what Johnny Miller has to say about the topic in *Pure Golf* (twelve pages or so on the grip). Miller advises that Hogan spent his whole life working on the swing and in the end he arrived at a neutral, palms-facing grip. Although this grip is regarded by many as too weak, Miller adds that it "is good enough for me," further describing it as the grip he will teach to his children. That is good enough for me!

Even when there is seeming agreement on grip fundamentals, there remains a wide difference of opinion regarding all manner of esoteric details, such as whether the golfer should use a long or short thumb. Hogan started with a long thumb but advocated a short-thumb position he adopted upon leaving the service in 1945, likely the product or reaction to his need to rein in loose aspects of his early swing, photographs of which bear a striking resemblance to the position at the top achieved by none other than John Daily. There is no consensus among modern-day golfers, either, including Tom Watson and Tom Kite, who have stated preferences for long or short thumbs, respectively. Instruction often cites similar rationale in support of the opposite viewpoint. David Leadbetter points this incongruity out in his exceptional book *The Fundamentals of Hogan*, namely that in his library of golf instruction there is no lack of support for opposite points of view that still manage to be integrated by their proponents into complete instruction systems. Leadbetter spends almost sixteen pages on the grip, but also sneaks in some grip recommendations or ramifications in other sections throughout his fine book. So much for the BFO of grip "fundamentals!"

A similar philosophical difference exists regarding the swing plane and the wisdom of employing a relatively flat plane, which many instructors erroneously associate with *Five Lessons*. Within the book, Hogan clearly states that characterizing a swing plane as flat or steep without consideration of the attributes of the golfer is wrong; he felt the plane should more properly be considered relative to the stature (e.g., height, length of arms and legs) of the golfer. He states plainly that there is no absolute and standard swing plane for all golfers. But there is a point beyond which swings should not venture or thereby risk ruinous effect, both above and below the angle or line formed by the head, shoulder, and ball line. Many instructors dispute this "fundamental" approach and insist that aligning in this manner results in too flat a swing plane, which causes a number of potential problems within the swing, not the least of which is a hook. Most beginners do not suffer this problem.

Two points about Hogan's admonition for the plane are germane. The primary reason that the plane was so important to Hogan is simply because of supination. It is at best very difficult, if not impossible to supinate properly with a swing plane that is too upright, which results in the hands (and therefore the clubface) entering the hitting zone in the wrong orientation in relation to the ideal or acceptable swing path through the ball. The upright swing plane requires some type of compensatory move entering the hitting area that renders problematic achieving the repeated, consistent action that Hogan sought. The second point regards Hogan's stature and the factoid contributed by Hogan photographer-extraordinaire Jules Alexander – that Hogan had a sleeve length of thirty-five inches, which is astoundingly long for his height. So his swing needed to be relatively flat in general. Other instructors take issue with the notion or construct of the swing as a "two-plane swing," believing that this adds unnecessary complexity to an already-complex maneuver.

A school of instruction exists touting a "one plane swing," with the late Moe Norman as its most famous practitioner or proponent. For those who have not heard of "Pipeline Moe," he is the exception to Hogan's premise that a straight ball is an accident. Hailing from Canada, he was an original character who made his mark through an uncanny ability to hit the golf ball straight. Stories abound regarding Moe. My favorite is one that describes how he hit shots off the putting green at Augusta one year to demonstrate how shallow his ball contact was. Can you imagine? He described his technique as hitting it on the "second groove" (You can search for and see footage of this legendary character on the Internet. It is worth the look). Others disputed the difference between the two planes described in Hogan's book. There were and are myriad debates about the positions and recommendations described as fundamentals within the book.

The notion that a firm understanding of the fundamentals was all that was required to play good golf and to break eighty was scoffed at by many reviewers. Too many of the so-called fundamentals were not roundly viewed as fundamentals at all, being somewhat variable and largely in dispute among instructors. This argument remains relevant. Although no serious golf instructor would focus on the swing of say, a Miller Barber, the legendary "Mr. X," for example, as an exemplar for the average golfer to swing a golf club, you could do worse than to focus on his ability to get on point through the box, e.g., his position coming into and through the hitting zone. The same with Jim Furyk's famous swing; despite the charge of looking like an octopus falling out of a tree, both his and Mr. X's swings are things of beauty through the hitting zone and from the more important standpoint of achieving results. They obviously have solid fundamentals and good grips, as well. I like the comment attributed to a golf instructor when he first observed the young Ben Crenshaw and what was viewed as an excessive head movement off the ball during the swing. He said, "I can tell you one thing; you never would have heard of Ben Crenshaw if I got a hold of him when he was younger." So much for fundamentals as panacea!

So the notion that the mission pursued by Hogan in 1946 centered on fixing his fundamentals as a way to fix his swing once and for all was likewise dismissed as evidence that he was withholding information or that he had a "secret" of some type. Hogan's efforts on the practice field indeed bore fruit in 1946. What he discovered, and the manner in which he implemented it, produced immediate, resounding, and lasting success, as evidenced by his golfing results. For the golfing public, bits and pieces of the story came out in the ensuing years, but it would be eight years until the 1954 *Life* magazine speculated about his by then famous secret, which Hogan went on to fully describe in the subsequent *Life* magazine article. His description of pronation and the twist that he gives his wrist at the top of the swing resulted in a technique that made his swing hook-proof. With this move added to his golf swing, he could not turn the clubface over before impact and he was unable to hook the ball. Hogan added an admonition that the secret would probably be of little-to-no use for the average golfer and would be ruinous for a poor golfer.

Others noted that this Scottish application employed to get the ball airborne often resulted in inducing, rather than preventing, a hook. Many also later observed that this topic was lightly treated in *Five Lessons*, with very little discussed about pronation at all, with the exception of a small part of the book that talked about the ruinous problems associated with early downswing pronation. But nothing of the hand twist and nothing of pronation on the backswing was covered until the updated foreword was added, capturing the 1984 discussion between Nick Seitz and Ben Hogan.

One of the problems resulting from this sequence of events is that many golfers who attempted the "secret" from 1955 found to their dismay that they struggled with consistency and did not find immediate gain from the application. Similarly, disputes continued about the wisdom of moving the hips as fast as Hogan recommended, because of the effect of flinging the arms about like a rag doll. The arms simply could not keep up in many swings. Golfers prone to slice the ball sliced even worse with the fundamentals applied the way he suggested. Additionally, the new and emerging stars of the golf world mostly had different-looking fundamentals, with upright-looking swings, reverse "Cs," "flying elbows," etc. Then again, there was Arnold Palmer.

Eventually, when Hogan offered to reveal his "real secret" for the right price, negotiations were reportedly begun for the next episode of the Hogan secret chronicles. Though figures were reportedly as high as one hundred thousand dollars, the deal never came to fruition. Many golfers and writers associated with the story were, needless to say, somewhat put off by the ensuing events. Many accused Hogan of stringing people along in his quest to get money for nothing. Even the normally light-opinioned Sam Snead weighed in at one point to say that "anybody can say he's got a secret if he won't tell what it is."

True to form, Hogan did not offer much in the way of a rebuttal to these insinuations. He often said that the only thing a man has is his name; if he somehow loses the respect, credibility, and reputation associated with his name, what does he have left? John Shlee quotes Hogan in *Maximum Golf* as telling him, in response to Shlee's request to use Hogan's name in association with his new golf school, that Hogan "had spent the better part of his life ensuring that his name would come up with adjectives that would please him." He encouraged Shlee to work on creating his own adjectives. Why did Hogan not take action on this little matter of the secret to continue the flow of adjectives that would please him?

This saga with the secret seems somewhat out of character for somebody who typically shunned attention away from the golf course, and who was not always portrayed in the best light by the media. The *Life* magazine article was probably understandable, as Hogan had a date with destiny once he first uttered the word "secret" as an explanation for his phenomenal play and results after 1946. Being the complicated individual he was, some of it may have been attributable to the lingering effects of his efforts to prove that he merited the same respect given to his long-time rival Byron Nelson. Byron's success during the war years had earned him a reputation as one of the "Gold Dust Twins" along with "Jug" McSpaden. Byron had also been referred to as "Mr. Golf" during the war years and throughout this period as a result of his phenomenal eleven straight victories and eighteen total wins in 1945, which reportedly and obviously bothered Hogan (e.g., Mr. Golf) quite a bit. When Byron was in the midst of a successful run for the Masters Championship of 1942, he insinuated that he had a secret he was using that was putting him over the top toward victory. Upon securing the title, he acknowledged that his secret was to ignore the pins and just shoot for the greens. This made for good copy for golf readers and Hogan must have noticed the attention paid to his rival. And of course, as noted previously, Byron was the number-one golfer in the MacGregor Golf Club stable.

But if Hogan had some other secret, why had he not revealed it when he "promised to do so" in the *Life* article? I believe that the reason he did not reveal his true secret has much to do with the above description of his concern for the adjectives raised in conjunction with his name. Regarding the *Life* article and *Five Lessons* in particular, I believe the main reason he did not reveal his "real secret" nor include it was simply because it was not a fundamental of the golf swing that would benefit any other golfer that did not have his action. To understand the reason for that in detail, we must return to that morning in 1946 when Ben Hogan went to the practice field to test out his latest theory on how to prevent a hook.

CHAPTER SEVEN

Digging it Out of the Dirt

"Reverse every natural instinct and do the opposite of what you are inclined to do, and you will probably come very close to having a perfect golf swing."
Ben Hogan

A number of people put Hogan's secret in context without revealing his actual secret. One of the most pointed explanations is indirectly offered by Jackie Burke, Jr., in his book, *It's Only a Game*. I don't know Mr. Burke, but his book clearly marks him to be a man of few words who chooses them carefully and with the benefit of the wisdom and judgment that comes from a full life. Burke has been in the arena and it shows. He notes that Hogan had "500 fundamentals" over his career and was working on one hundred at any one moment. Some lasted throughout his career and some were discarded the second they were proven inadequate. The ones that worked stuck, the proof or litmus being that they were integrated into his swing. Further, the techniques peculiar to Hogan's swing or Burke's, for that matter, were germane to him but might not even be applicable to you or another golfer. The bottom line is that, just because a golfer says it is a fundamental, does not make it so – whether it is Hogan, some guru, or me (which highlights his point, since I obviously don't belong in this reference.) I assume he would agree with my caveat for clarity purposes, offered in a similar manner to the clarifications he made for some of his famous father's recommendations, the phrase I like to apply: "all things being equal."

Back to the prelude to the practice field, and we find Hogan, having taken time off, desperate and puzzling over the details of what he could do to change his tendency to hook. Hogan noted on a number of occasions that he thought about the problem for several days, when the concept of the old Scottish technique of pronation came to him. He may have tried it a time or two in the past before he had solidified the importance of the plane to his swing action. He apparently worked it out in his mind and resolved to try it to see if his theory was correct that a cupped-wrist position at the top of the swing would indeed prevent him from hooking. His past efforts to weaken his grip and thereby mitigate to the greatest extent possible, while not totally eliminating the threat of hitting a hook, had largely resulted in a narrowing of the window of acceptability to contact the golf ball beyond the point where it was sustainable – even for a perfectionist who practiced and played as much as humanly possible. His efforts had resolved to a point where his margin of error on his shot making was so minuscule that few other golfers could have functioned under the constraints.

There is a picture of the face of his famous one-iron and the wear pattern or ball mark is so close to the hosel that it is startling to think of the precision it took to hit that club, particularly under pressure. The footage of Hogan's ball-striking during this period gives the impression that his swing-plane arc worked deliberately from outside to inside, cutting across the ball, yet producing a straight shot, intersecting with the ball for the briefest of milliseconds, making contact and the influence on the ball even less brief. This was quite unlike his later technique, where he had a discernable movement to and through the ball from the inside to outside, exhibiting a "chase movement" somewhat down the line, but moving quickly left or inward after contact, vice the glancing blow characterized above that was an outside to inside movement. This later look to his impact zone action was characterized by David Leadbetter in *The Fundamentals of Hogan* as approaching from the inside but moving sharply inside or left after impact.

Hogan's critical self-assessment was focused on resolving this matter in a way that would free his action from the confines of the corner he had painted himself into through a systematic and somewhat dogmatic compensation to his fundamental swing. His analysis no doubt included a review of his play and his results for the past several years, as well as a review of all aspects of his game, to include his clubs. He was in a continuous contest with McGregor, his golf club sponsor throughout this portion of his career. He was reportedly somewhat miffed about not being the top golfer in the stable, which was occupied by Byron Nelson, and also irate at their continued inability to set up his clubs to his specification. So he relooked at his clubs and made some adjustments where necessary to facilitate his objective.

Among the fundamentals he counted upon was having an extremely stiff shaft in his clubs to minimize the shaft flex so that he did not have to wrestle with that variable element or more to the theory of keeping the variables to a minimum. He built up his grips even more so than usual, to a thickness that inhibited the rolling or release of the wrists as a way to prevent the clubface from closing too early or at all before impact. He flattened his lies so he could stay below the plane and not risk coming over the top or restricting his release by coming into the ball too steeply, and he weakened his lofts a bit to open the clubface even more. The resulting look to his golf clubs was similar in appearance to the look of a hockey stick. And he worked on achieving a consistent pronation movement to the top of the swing similar to that outlined later in the *Life* magazine article. The initial movement was a relatively small amount of wrist cock; that is a "fanning open" or clockwise rolling or opening of the clubface to get a fairly consistent wrist cup position at the top of the swing.

Hogan probably resolved to work his knockdown-drill swing to ensure consistency in application, later outlined in *Five Lessons*. The point of the drill was to link the arms to the body and also to synchronize the movement of the lower and upper body. He had already gone to a shortened thumb position when he left the service. He states that he further committed to modifying his grip by moving his left-hand grip a bit farther to the left than before, as he describes in *Five Lessons*, almost a full inch. This placed his right and left hand "Vs" in a position where they were literally pointing straight at the button of his chin.

Finally, he resolved that drastic measures were called for to ensure that he would not have to repeat this effort again in a few years or that he would settle for a quick fix when he in fact needed more serious work. I can't overstress the point: Hogan was desperate to find a way to resolve the problem; he was a belt-and-suspenders guy, that is, prone to overkill in the application of a fix and he believed he would never compete in the majors if he did not fix his hooking problem. Having spent several days thinking about it and resolving upon a course of action, he decided that he needed to take drastic and bold action and he had just the thing in mind to do.

Hogan's account states that the idea of pronation came to him suddenly one morning. But I believe what actually came to him that morning, as desperate as he was to find a fix, was the idea of thinking through what a golfer with the opposite problem, that is a slicer, would do. And if he could work through the trials that a golfer with the opposite problem would suffer, through a process that resulted in hooking the ball, then the transition point from slice to hook should allow him to do the same thing going the other way. After all, he spent the better part of the previous fourteen years trying to work the problem the other way and curing a hook with limited success.

With all the plans and changes in place, there was only one thing left for Hogan to do to ensure that his trial on the practice tee would be credible, that it would present a dramatic contrast to his normal efforts, and that he would not simply repeat his faulty approach that had proven insufficient in previous efforts. In the past he had simply worked harder at what he was doing, rather than try to approach it differently and work it smarter. He always believed the answers he was looking for could be found through hard work, that he could dig it out of the dirt. This problem had long defied that notion and his efforts had only served to limit his available courses of action through implementation of defensive measures, rather than solving his basic problem of hooking.

He was so serious about finding a solution that he took time off and didn't touch a club for several days. He wanted something that was certain to work, not just another patch of the problem that would have to be fixed again in six months. But when he needed to work on something different or when he was having a little skittles match or an on course practice game against himself by playing as many as three balls, left, right and center, he often called on his counter point, test golfer, or "alter ego," Henny Bogan, to play the anti-Ben Hogan part. If Hogan was playing conservatively and trying to post a score on his ball at a new course, Henny would take the aggressive line to test the alternative path to the green. And vice versa, if Hogan was the master of course management tactics and positional golf, Henny was the anti-master, immune to even the thought of playing smartly.

Hogan was methodical and deliberate in the way he went about the pursuit of even the slightest change to his golf swing. He honed the technique to a razor's edge over the years as he went about changing his swing a little piece at a time, simultaneously staying competitive week after week during the pro tournaments. Henny was a construct in keeping with that methodology and the practice technique was much more of a lark than anything deeper, but it also provided for a pleasant distraction to keep him interested in the game while helping him to achieve a meaningful separation of his methods and trials. Hogan was more scientist than golfer when he set about the business of testing new techniques, clubs or a hypothesis for better play. Henny, as a practice construct, allowed him to work in relative privacy on swing changes, experimental techniques and, more importantly, to hone his concentration; again there was likely nothing deeper or more meaningful about it. His powers of concentration were extraordinary enough that he could do a meaningful separation in this manner of technique, all without having to suffer (relatively speaking) playing partners who all too often were prone to gab or simply weren't serious enough about their golf games. No "jolly" golf was ever played in these sessions. As it turned out, Henny Bogan's role in this endeavor turned out to be the critical element.

The man who actually took to the practice field that spring morning of 1946 was a miserable soul named Henny Bogan. He was the anti-Ben Hogan; and he was miserable because, unlike Ben Hogan, he could not hook the ball. Everyone knows that good players struggle with a hook, and the better they get, the more they struggle. Well, Henny Bogan was a pitiable hack who suffered from a slice; he was simply incapable of hooking the ball. Henny was desperate to cure his slice, as desperate as Hogan was about his hook. Henny desired nothing more in this world than to learn to hook the ball, but he had always struggled with that aspect of his game. With his thick grips, weakened lofts, flat lies, stiffened shafts, an extremely weak grip, and a pronation move in his backswing, he struggled to fade the ball and not slice uncontrollably, never mind to hit a good player shot like a hook.

Henny took to the field and since he was the anti-Ben Hogan, he likely did everything the opposite of what Hogan would have done to ensure the experiment was credible. Hogan was always neatly dressed in earth tones and good-looking golf attire; Henny was an unshaven, fashion nightmare. Hogan wore his trademark cap that came to be associated with him; Henny wore a cockeyed ball cap or the same cloth hat but lacked the knowledge of how to properly wear it. Hogan normally started with a nine-iron to hit warm up shots; Henny started with the long clubs. Hogan had a relatively closed, narrow stance with the longer clubs; Henny's was wide open and wide apart. Hogan had a relatively weak grip; Henny's grip had been modified so it was extremely weak to the point where it was difficult if not impossible to square the clubface. Hogan hit a shot that tended to go right to left, a draw or a hook, with every club; Henny faded or sliced every club. Hogan had a precise backswing plane with a flat wrist that stayed on that plane; Henny "pronated." He had an odd bow or a cup in his wrist that forced the swing plane to move somewhat upward and out of position as he swung. Hogan aimed right of the target and drew it well back to the target; Henny aimed left of the target and faded or sliced it back to the target. Ben Hogan's mental image of Henny Bogan is more like the picture on page twenty-two of *Ben Hogan: The Man Behind The Mystique* by Martin Davis.

With regard to Henny, we are talking about a golfer who was desperate to change his natural tendency of slicing – as desperate as Hogan was to cure his hook, and as desperate as a person can be who feels they are pursuing an issue that will determine their very golfing life. But if Henny could somehow make his slice into a fade, and his fade into a draw, then a golfer looking to work the transition the other way might learn something of value.

When Henny hit the first couple of shots, they probably faded or sliced quite a bit, since everything about his fundamentals oriented to that shot outcome. After all, that was his problem and the reason he was there in the first place. But Henny was being coached by none other than the great Ben Hogan, who, sincere in his efforts to help Henny, adjusted his stance and swing as he progressed through the bag to fine tune his position to help him reduce the slice to a fade and to help him draw the ball. While Henny may have been a hack because of his slicing issues, there were some standards applied, and the eye of the master was upon him, helping.

These warm-up shots were probably consistent with documented video evidence released in recent years that show Hogan with a parallel stance with everything largely aligned along traditional lines, e.g., parallel left with regard to the clubface, but with the clubface offset or aimed slightly right of a line that would be considered classicly parallel. Many of these videos were not captured from the center point and are therefore not oriented properly on a reliable line to gauge the positions definitively. But there are enough videos available to generalize the positions. The hip-to-hip practice drill outlined in *Five Lessons* is this swing. Hogan's swing objective throughout his golfing life from a very early age (adopted to gain distance) was based upon the premise of timing the turn of his hips with the launching or release of his arms toward impact, to leverage the free ride of the arms, caused by the first transition movement leftward, to position the elbows (particularly the right) off his hip – ready to be propelled to a closed position through impact by the turn of the right hip. It was a move he perfected as a caddy when he was busy competing for nickels at Glen Garden with the other caddies in the early to mid-1920s. The loser had to shag all the balls for the others. His goal was to position the right elbow and arm as if to throw a punch toward the outer portion of the golf ball; the arm never made it closed unless the left hand stopped, slowed or broke down, but his objective was to close it nonetheless. The caddy or target is at the mid-point or twelve o'clock position. Adopting this stance or position, he later warmed up his swing action by hitting the nine-iron and swinging to a nine o'clock or a left arm parallel to the ground position, hitting knockdowns or seventy-five-percent power shots. The ball contact looks almost thin with a distinctly toe bias impression. The action takes place so fast we must base our observations on impressions, thus, the caveats; nonetheless, there is a distinct impression of ball contact toward the toe.

  While the main purpose of this swing is to warm up and lubricate the body and to mobilize the moving parts, the primary purpose is to synchronize the movement of the pieces and the parts keyed off the turn of the hips, while re-establishing how little effort is required to hit the ball if everything is synchronized properly. Hogan's main objective throughout his golfing life (again) was to synchronize his swing but, to put a finer point on it, for his arms and his release to keep pace with the turn of the hips. So this drill focused on the lower and upper body while working on the adhesion of the arms to the sides, while ingraining the proper feel of the use of the hands by totally eliminating any conscious hand action *prior to impact* other than that caused by supination. Not to isolate supination, per se, but to refresh the proper feel of the slinging effect being transferred to the hands, that is achieved through the whipsaw-like action of the arms being pulled or "elongated" off the left side and propelled off the turn of the hip on the right side. Being positioned at the end of the arms, the hands supinate in a quite unconscious way, as demands are placed upon them by the transfer of energy between the lower body, hips, shoulders, and arms. They are a captive audience forced to obey the principal of centrifugal – or more appropriately in Hogan's case – with pronation: centripetal force. This drill will not work properly with an upright swing plane without some type of swing compensation.

With Henny set up to hit warm-up shots, a*ll things being equal,* there was little-to-no possibility that he could close the clubface prematurely or before impact. So there was little possibility that a hook could result from this position with his weak fundamentals. That was obviously the case to be worked on that day. The normal ball flight and distance achieved from this position with a nine o'clock swing is a straight-flighted, lower-trajectory ball with less spin that goes roughly seventy-five percent or, roughly, two clubs less than a normal shot.

The distances published in *Power Golf* for Hogan's clubs roughly corresponds to this formula when you consider a maximum or full (normal) swing, an average or ten-thirty (three quarters of the way back) position and a minimum or nine o'clock (halfway back) swing position. Some have trouble translating swings to clock positions, but in simple terms the nine o'clock position has the lead arm parallel to the ground, whereas the ten-thirty position is halfway between parallel and fully extended skyward behind you. The time references are close enough as an exemplar for the referenced swings and, more to the point, Hogan's game depended on consistently reaching the same positions time after time, exactly alike from shot to shot and club to club. There are many exemplar photographs of Hogan in these positions.

Coupled with a cupped or pronated wrist in his swing, Hogan reached a position on the backswing where there was no chance that his clubface could possibly close prior to impact short of a "lightning-like" amateur-style move at the bottom of his swing. I would venture that most of us golfers have never been in this position in our golfing lives; further, many have difficulty envisioning how Hogan himself managed to get the club head back to the ball in time from this position. Hogan worked to attain this position time after time, knowing that the release of the pent-up force of the big muscles would propel the little muscles with such force, which translates to speed as they achieve the correct position, forcing the left hand through the supination sequence just in time to contact the ball, in keeping with the model of the ideal swing.

Hogan was able to achieve these positions through extraordinary hand and wrist strength, flexibility, exceptional timing, and concentration. Hogan's position was precise enough to set your watch by, as they say, as only Hogan could make them. Of the tens of millions of golfers who have looked to and read *Five Lessons* over the years, there is not one in ten thousand (and it may be lower than that) who comes away with the correct impression of how Hogan swung the golf club and how he intended us to go about it using the inside muscles. He indicates how different his action is by reference to the wear pattern (callous) of his hands. Hogan does not stress the point and most golfers and golf writers have either totally ignored this figure or have found it as yet another example of a dogmatic approach. A golfer who uses the inside muscles properly will swing the club in a manner that will produce a sling or a fling of the ball, with the resulting wrench or tug on the left arm producing a similar callous pattern, including a callous on the inside of the ring finger. Most golfers move through supination but do not use the inside muscles as Hogan stressed and advocated.

I have always found the photographs of Hogan in these positions to be extraordinary, as it is the pictorial epitome of the feel of the swing that I describe elsewhere in the book as my long-sought-after vision of my Tournament Players Club Starr Pass experience. These positions were quite foreign to those found in my golf swing in 1991 when I began my own quest to improve my swing.

Henny probably hit some pretty good benders, even with a knockdown action, because supination combined with his weak grip meant he could not possibly square the clubface. The goal with this drill later became, as stated above, to isolate the feel of the club head literally sliding under the ball to sling it at the target, and Henny probably had to make some fairly major adjustments to ensure he didn't slice it off the map. Many of the defensive moves that Hogan had experimented with over the years involved cutting somewhat across the ball from the outside, which had to be modified considerably to reduce and eliminate the slicing action. The natural tendency of the body and the mind (or from a swing thought perspective with this approach, because one is trying to hit a fade), is to think of the action as one moving outside to inside. One of the first fairly major adjustments done that day was to swing more from a neutral or inside position, as anything else produced a serious slice.

Most who have tried this technique (a so-called body release) will appreciate how easy it is to block the ball to a two o'clock position even without a reasonably weak grip. After all, the desire wasn't just to prevent Henny from slicing, but was actually focused on helping him hit a hook. Henny got bolder and bolder as his inability to hook the ball no matter what he did made him increasingly anxious about what it would take to hit an actual draw. The more he tried to draw the ball by swinging more and more from an inside path, the higher and farther he hit it, and the less he was slicing it, and the more he was fading it. Many of the balls flew as if pulled, but basically went straight, particularly for a golfer accustomed to seeing slices (or draws).

As Hogan made adjustments to Henny's stance to accommodate the ball flight and adjusted his aim point based on the results of his shots, he found that he was hitting the ball as well as he had ever hit it in his life. The more he tried to hook it by emphasizing the inside path, the more consistent the ball flight became until, much like artillery fire, he literally walked it on to the target by moving his aim point. He no doubt started by aiming quite a bit left of the target to fade it back, but found himself moving it continuously farther and farther right as the optimal aim point position resolved that way. The more Henny focused on hooking the ball, the more he produced not quite draws or hooks, but pulls or slings, relatively straight balls that moved right as they fell toward the target. At some point Henny added enough right-hand action to feel that he was literally making the proper hook action that Hogan wanted, in fact just like Hogan, but with a pronated or cupped left wrist. He eventually made so many small adjustments that he reached the transition point, where his stance was closed much more than would ever be practical on the golf course, and yet he was still unable to hook! In fact, he began to slice again!

The best he could hit was the pull or block, but it still trailed right at the end toward the target. At the transition point, the adjustments were so acute and his stance was so closed, he starting slicing anew rather than just fading the ball (because all things were equal). He eventually settled for an aim point around thirty degrees offset right from the actual target, which was centered between the aim point and the line of Henny's body, which was aligned about thirty degrees left of the target and slightly open with the shorter clubs, about the same, but with a closed stance for the mid-to-longer clubs. So the clubface was actually aimed somewhat right of a normal position at about one o'clock and slightly open; the target line was at twelve o'clock or somewhat left of the aim point; the body line was aligned at eleven o'clock. The line to the target was a bit off parallel to the aim point of the clubface, and the line of the body was aligned a bit off parallel to the target line. But the line of the body was not aligned parallel to the aim of the clubface, which looked slightly right. Modifications right of this point, all things being equal, produced more fade. Hitting the ball at less than full force also produced more fade.

The harder Henny tried to hook the ball, using his best imitation of a Hogan-like action (but with the wrist cupped), the higher and straighter the ball flew. Henny was eventually doing the opposite of what he thought he should do, that is, he was pronating his wrist with the expectation of fading the ball while trying desperately to hook the ball and truly emphasizing the inside-to-out swing path that should have produced a draw, at the very least. He was violating his body's natural tendency to swing from outside to inside, to make what should have been a fade-swing technique, by increasingly making a draw swing that looked more and more like Hogan by the swing. The harder he hit it, the straighter the ball went.

The odd part about it was that while Henny was trying unsuccessfully to hit a hook, he was actually aiming right of the target and pulling or slinging or blocking the ball to the left. But it was clearly not a hook at all, in fact, the predominate ball flight was distinctively tailing or fading to the right as it fell nearly straight down from an apex that was quite unlike his normal ball flight. Despite his best efforts, he could not get much of a movement from right to left; to the contrary, the predominate movement remained left to right, and the modulation that could be controlled through the stance was the amount of movement, but not the basic flight. When he attempted to add more pronation by rolling the clubface open faster, the ball went higher and straighter (as Hogan later related to Nick Seitz in *Five Lessons*) than before. In fact, the harder he hit it, the straighter it went! This remained true no matter how much pronation was added. The more aggressively the pronation move was applied, all things being equal, the higher and straighter the ball went. This point totally bypassed Henny in his frustration at not being able to hit the hook he desired, namely the fact that he was a slicer who was aiming right of the target (not left). If he let up somewhat and did not hit the ball hard, the ball moved quite a bit from left to right.

At some point in the practice session, it became apparent that Henny was indeed a hack and was unable to draw the ball much if any; he certainly could not hook the ball. He was swinging pretty much exactly like Hogan by this point, attempting to hit a hook with the same action. But with all things being equal, including the base fundamentals, coupled with pronation, he could not move it right to left. Even when he pulled the ball, it faded at the end. The only way a hook was going to be hit was to let Hogan hit a few shots, drop the pronation or the bowed wrist entirely, and let Ben Hogan show him how to do it. The experiment for Henny was proving to be a failure and did not bode well for the desperate Hogan at this point, since his entire premise that morning was predicated upon using what Henny learned as the point of departure for his own efforts, albeit, then focused on the anti-Henny proposition. But if Henny was unable to cross over, that is to get to the point where his slice became a fade and then a draw, and his draw became a hook, Hogan would not get the information he was looking for to help him traverse the opposite direction with his own swing. Hogan decided to give Henny a rest at some point and to reaffirm where he was at in the process by re-base-lining things by hitting some shots with his normal swing.

When Ben Hogan dropped the pronation move and hit a couple of shots, he had what I have described as an "Aha moment." The subtlety that bypassed Henny in his quest to draw or to hook was not long lost on Ben Hogan, that is, the fact that a slicer was aiming to the right of the target without the fear of the ball going further right. He was probably dumbstruck at how simple the solution was and how long it had taken him to discover something that was right there to be found. With the stance and alignment he had worked out to adjust and shift Henny's ball flight toward the target, Hogan's ball flight made a perfect arc toward the same target with the same exceptional results. The difference from Hogan's normal shot being the fact that the draw action was all done well to the right of and to the target, rather than being equal measures right and left, but from the same basic stance, setup, and swing. The only real or substantive differences at this point between Henny and Hogan's action and swing were the pronation or cupped wrist. Stripped bare of all the defensive moves that Hogan added over the years, the swing was simply his normal action that produced a draw or hook every time, a swing he had perfected over twenty years or more starting with his caddy days. Hogan found that the more he tried to hit a big draw or borderline hook, the farther right or outside the target line the ball flew, but with very little hook action left of the target. The only way to produce a shot that would move well left of the target was to aim improperly; no amount of effort to swing harder caused the problem that had plagued him for nearly two decades.

Alternating between Henny pronation shots and Hogan regular-swing practice shots verified the importance of the plane to facilitate a full and proper release. In fact the only way Henny could hook the ball with a cupped wrist is if he totally violated fundamentals by straightening his right arm by moving it off his hip early, or by shattering the pane of glass on his backswing and coming over the top. The same proved true for Hogan; the only way he could induce a slice or a hook that swung wide of the target violently was to similarly violate one of his fundamentals by getting his weight on his toes, or allowing his right arm to leave his side, or getting upright with his plane, or by aiming improperly, or by hitting early and making a bad swing. Or ironically enough, to add one of the defensive moves he had employed for the better part of a decade. In other words, if Hogan followed the natural tendency of either his body or his mind, it resulted in a bad shot. Hogan was not in the habit of producing those types of shots on a whim, but he surely found it ironic that many of the supposed "cures" he had applied were precisely the wrong medicine at the wrong time and exacerbated or extended his struggles. When he added the pronation move but did not swing hard, the ball faded quite a bit. With pronation and a hard or full swing, the ball tended to go straight or with a slight fade at the end. The big difference from his previous attempts was attempting to hit a fade using his normal action, that is a swing with a draw action from the inside, using the same stance, alignment, and technique. His previous efforts were thwarted somewhat by his defensive changes to his swing, many of which based on the opposite swing path, that is from outside to inside. Swinging that way was a natural reaction to his hooking problems that had set him back considerably in terms of finding alternatives. The only difference between his swing action now, (when he wanted to fade the ball rather than hook it), was the application of the pronation move. His previous efforts implemented via the weakened grip focused on a fade-swing thought and a fade-swing action that cut across the ball from the outside, as opposed to his normal action that went from inside to out. Who would believe that the way to achieve his goal was to hook his fades, confident in the knowledge that pronation would prevent hitting a hook?

Hogan had to sit down to think through where he had arrived with his efforts. He must have been dumbfounded and distrustful that he had stumbled onto the correct technique by doing something that somehow never occurred to him to try in the previous fourteen years, as it was the opposite of what made sense to do. It was so absolutely counter-intuitive and preposterous that it could have been that simple all along, and yet he had not thought to try it.

Henny left that day totally frustrated, having only hit a few draws, the result of improper swing planes, weight too far forward, or just plain bad swings. Henny was the hack that Hogan knew him to be; he was incapable of playing a good players shot. Hogan left ecstatic and full of hope for the next day. I doubt he slept a wink that night for fear that something or someone or some event would ruin his chances to repeat the events of that day. Or that he would wake up and find out that it was a delusion, dream, or result of something else he had found that was a "one-day wonder." He probably finished chronicling the events of the day in his notebook; this information later served as more feeder material or the foundation for *Five Lessons*.

When he returned to the practice tee the next day he fine-tuned the details even more, but he achieved the same results. It is hard to imagine how he must have felt. It had been more than two decades of work, counting the time from his first swing adjustment at age thirteen, encompassing almost fifteen years as a professional golfer, all the while living with a self-described rattlesnake in his golf bag. All the work he had done over the years, including the practice time, the sacrifice of his time and the expenditure of energy culminated in his solving the puzzle he had been working on all that time. Words cannot express the joy and sense of relief that Hogan must have felt when he left the practice field that second day. He had finally dug the answer out of the dirt!

In the final analysis, Henny Bogan never did learn to hook, as his best efforts to make a good golfers swing from inside to outside with a pronating motion proved immune to "rattlesnakes." The only way he found he could hit the ball right to left was to let Ben Hogan hit those shots. And Ben Hogan learned to fade the ball from a hack who could not even hit a professional shot, namely a draw. The delicious irony of the whole thing is that Ben Hogan learned how to fade the ball by trying to hook every shot! Put a different way, Hogan learned how to cure his hooking problems by hitting a hook! Again, this is why the phrase "all things being equal" is so important. As long as Hogan stayed true to his fundamentals as he described them in *Five Lessons*, then all things now being equal, he could aggressively go after the ball with his normal swing without fear of a hook, augmented with the following additional caveats:

1. Use extra thick grips to prevent excessive hand action (with reminder rib).
2. Employ a weakened grip to prevent turning over the clubface.
3. Use flattened lies that gave his clubs a "hockey stick" appearance to his relatively flat swing plane and his delayed hitting action.
4. Use weakened lofts so the clubface was already somewhat open at address.
5. Use very stiff shafts so there was no or minimal deflection as torque was applied.
6. Employ a backswing that aligned his swing plane with the shoulder-ball line as represented by keeping his shoulders and forearms below his image of the pane of glass.
7. Use an aim point about one o'clock or thirty degrees or so right of the target, with the target line and the body aligned appropriately left.
8. Apply his Henny Bogan pronation move.

In fact he found with practice that he could not hit the ball left at all unless he did something wrong! He could pour as much right side into the swing as he wanted, because he would not lose the supination move of the left hand, which was actually accentuated through impact by pronation and the concomitant unfolding or bowing or the "uncupping" move of his wrist (all things being equal.) Hogan's dogmatic application of the right fundamentals and positions meant that he repeated them every time and he was therefore always in a perfect position to accept (through supination) the application of right-side, right-hand power without breaking down. He added a reminder rib to his grips to ensure that he set his hands properly on the club each time. Hogan famously observed that golf and tournament golf are as different as "tennis and ice hockey." So the only thing left to do was to take on the baptism of fire, that is, to apply his newfound technique "under the gun" of tournament golf. The rest of the story, as they say, is history.

CHAPTER EIGHT

Implications

"I'm the sole judge of my standards."
Ben Hogan

Hogan left the practice field that spring of 1946 with no peer as far as ball-striking goes. He was already playing pretty consistent golf before this point in his career. But his results after this session speak for themselves. He often estimated that he saved a shot a round, minimum, through the application of his technique, but the boost to his confidence and consistency were obviously priceless. He had also added capability to his arsenal, namely the ability to hit targets calling for a left-to-right or fade ball flight. The methodology by which he achieved his secret speaks volumes, in hindsight, on the difficulty he had relating his technique to others over the ensuing five decades. I previously related that Hogan often paused for uncomfortably long periods of time when asked a question; this was due to his need to recreate the feel of the particular technique and then translate it from "Henny Bogan" speak to be usable for the golfer asking the question. He was obviously mindful of describing the application of his hooking action to produce the power fade that he became so famously associated with. Put a different way, how confusing would it have been for golfers if Hogan described his famous power fade as the product of an attempt to hook the ball? As he stated many times, his secret was easy to discover if he told you where to look – which was inside his head!

On the heels of his "aha moment" Hogan came to observe that by 1946 he "stopped trying to do a great number of things perfectly," because he had found that "such a focus on perfection was just not realistic or even necessary." We now know what he meant. His effort to dig the solution out of the dirt had resulted in the discovery that he could simply take his normal swing with a slight modification, on every shot, that is, pronation. We also know what he meant about doing things the opposite of the body's normal tendency. He spent almost eight years suppressing his natural tendency to apply his hook action through impact in favor of a fade technique and a swing thought that worked from the outside to the inside. With less focus on all things trivial, he reduced his true fundamentals down to a manageable seventeen or so by my count. This still probably sounds like a lot in comparison to the eight outlined in *Five Lessons*, particularly if you check-list them as you play before each shot. By his own admission, such was clearly not the case. The majority of the fundamentals had to do with either pre-swing activity or setup actions.

The basic fundamentals were listed in the previous chapter, including

1. Use extra thick grips to prevent excessive hand action (with reminder rib).
2. Employ a weakened grip to prevent turning over the clubface.
3. Use flattened lies that gave his clubs a "hockey stick" appearance to his relatively flat swing plane and his delayed hitting action.
4. Use weakened lofts so the clubface was already somewhat open at address.
5. Use very stiff shafts so there was no or minimal deflection as torque was applied.
6. Employ a backswing that aligned his swing plane with the shoulder-ball line as represented by keeping his shoulders and forearms below his image of the plane of glass.
7. Use an aim point about one o'clock or thirty degrees or so right of the target, with the target line and the body aligned appropriately left.

8. Apply his Henny Bogan pronation move.

To add the swing-related fundamentals of *Five Lessons*, the eight or nine are listed, which include:

(1) proper grip, including the correct stance and correct posture;

(2) proper waggle (which is how Hogan established the correct path back based on the shot he planned to play – to pre-set proper supination);

(3) starting the swing back with hands, arms, and shoulders, in that order;

(4) staying on the proper plane;

(5) reaching the correct position at the top of the backswing;

(6) initiating the downswing by turning the hips to the left;

(7) hitting through in one cohesive movement with the hips, shoulders, arms, and hands, in that order;

(8) starting to supinate the wrist at impact; and

(9) swinging through from the inside to outside to the finish.

Add to this list his course-management fundamentals, and you still have a greater number of items than the average human can effectively wrestle with; but these represented a considerable reduction for Hogan.

The course-management fundamentals are lightly touched upon in several references. For instance, taking more club and a lower trajectory to a back pin, or less club and a higher trajectory shot for a front pin. Adding the appropriate spin to the ball for the shot shape and approach chosen, e.g., left or right; and different playing styles for the weather, including wind, rain, dry conditions, etc.

There was an entire laundry list of items similar to this for his course-management approach. Much as Jackie Burke, Jr. noted, Hogan had hundreds of fundamentals at any one time. But having these basic items correct cleared the way for him to focus on golf-course management, envisioning shots, taking in the elements, producing shots, playing golf, and posting scores. Besides, he had just removed a number of items from the inventory he had learned over the years that went with his fade-swing thought. He no longer needed them. Most of the fundamental elements never literally made it onto the course with him, as they were second nature or setup items that he practiced so frequently they were like golf clothes. He never gave a passing thought to the elements as he initiated his pre-shot routine and went through the process he followed to hit the ball.

The fundamentals are obviously the items to focus on in practice. On the course, Hogan observed that he only needed to actively monitor five key items by his own accounts, although he later stated that he never had to re-look at or check more than the first two when there was a problem, or if he needed a tweak in the event that he hit a bad shot. These five key items most likely constituted the source and inspiration for his book. Because of his unique action, his five keys were in a different order of importance, with the plane and his right-side action, particularly the right elbow, the ones he paid closest attention to, although weight distribution was of equal importance. Despite it being attributed to him that he rarely hit more than three shots a round exactly as he planned them, most of his bad shots were clearly known only to him. Once he figured out the elements of the shot he wanted to hit, he executed the correct technique and went on about his business. And that technique involved him making the same basic swing he had been grooving since he was a caddy, only without the concern about hitting the ball left.

He spoke of having a wall down the left side of the golf course and being supremely confident that there was no chance of hitting it beyond that wall. Do we need to speculate further upon what his newfound confidence was based? How confident would you be if you had a base technique that you were absolutely positive about applying with no doubts whatsoever? Would that help out with your scores and your results?

Where Hogan ended up in his quest, that is, with the answers he was looking for all along, convinced him that all the activity that went before it was spent grooving a faulty swing. He said as much when he mused in *Five Lessons* about what a long time he had been in the business and how far he had taken the science of the swing. And how he would have liked to have started his investigation from where he ended up – with complete understanding of base fundamentals.

For him the trials and tribulations were unavoidable, but we can avoid much of the trouble by focusing, as Hogan recommended, on the true fundamentals. *Five Lessons* was his thoughtful effort to help others avoid those struggles, almost in the context of a gift to the golfing public, representing nearly three decades of his struggles to dig it out of the dirt.

CHAPTER NINE

Now that we know...

"It's not the amount of practice that helps reach your goal;
it's the right kind of practice."
Matthew Mills

Hogan was a talented, skilled, dedicated golf practitioner who spent the majority of his waking hours perfecting his swing. I mentioned earlier that he labored over fourteen years and hit an estimated several million balls through 1946 until he accomplished his goal. I'm restating those facts to put in perspective the "Pollyanna-like" optimism of the new or "average" golfer who expects to play fairly decent golf the odd three or four times a year they tee it up, while puzzling over the reason they don't do better at the game.

Before I decided to improve my golf, I expected to hit decent shots the eight or nine times a year that I played, but I knew it was unrealistic, given the lack of time I spent practicing. But I had a fairly decent natural golf swing and I played other sports, so the concept (golf) was not totally foreign. I had big expectations when I played. Other sports I played over the years included: baseball (shortstop and pitcher), softball, bowling, racquetball, Tae Kwon Do, tennis, mountain-biking, hockey, shooting (targets, not animals), and broomball. I also took the plunge to pursue my interest in music by taking guitar lessons (for anyone who is struck by the incongruity of including the guitar under a listing of sports, I would invite you to visit and view Matthew Mills neoclassical guitar videos on the Internet. The physicality engendered in the neoclassical style is, as world-famous Shred-Lord Joe Stump says, "Like your mother used to shred." You have to see it to believe it.)

I have trophies from participation in the majority of these sports and I consider myself athletic and somewhat quick to learn sports concepts, while readily admitting it is not a criterion to stand out among the sharp objects in the drawer. I approached the improvement of my golf game over some eighteen years or so in a methodical, albeit part-time manner, working to master the fundamentals, translated to mastery of my own swing. It took quite a while to work things out on my own and I have yet to translate that knowledge to consistent play on the golf course. I will later describe the path I followed, but my main point is that I was looking to improve my swing as the primary motivation for my efforts, and I was stubborn enough to believe that I was smart and athletic enough to figure it out if I just kept at it in a methodical way. I suffered through periods of lousy golf over the years to stay on what I thought was a clear development path, often having difficulty getting my golf game from the practice tee to the course. I was not trying to solve any secrets, per se, but I increasingly focused on trying to figure out why I could not translate the fundamentals outlined within *Five Lessons* directly into better play.

My efforts increasingly constituted a continual revisit of the concepts outlined within *Five Lessons* until I finally reached the point where I got them right in the summer of 2008. It took me that long to work it out on my own, and I think the biggest lesson learned from my efforts is that golf is a deceptively difficult sport where the body's natural instincts and tendencies work against you each step of the way. All this is to say that getting professional help to learn golf is a very good idea.

The only years I played a lot of golf after I retired from the military in 1994 was a three-year period when I played more than twenty rounds of golf each year. Other than that, I played sporadically, mostly scrambles, but I practiced with the consistent objective of working to improve my swing, rather than my score. If you are a new golfer or if you know a golfer who is either learning to play or is passionate about playing but frequently complains or stresses how they would like to improve, you could do that person a huge favor by buying him or her a five-lesson package with a local pro from a nearby golf course for the holidays, birthday, Groundhog Day, or whatever. The best time to do it is at the onset of golf fever when the first discussion about doing better with your own clubs starts. Trust me on this one; your friend will love you for it! Most will likely never do it for themselves; it is against human nature to seek out help like this – and that somehow goes double for new golfers. You can simply say that you read at the grocery store or in an airline magazine or somewhere credible that the average golf handicap in America is around a fifteen or eighteen for both sexes and it hasn't changed in twenty years or so, despite the improvements in technology; and you read somewhere else that any person with average athletic ability should be able to break eighty within a year or so, all things being equal (ATBE); and you figured out that ATBE means having sound fundamentals. If your friends are athletic, all you need to add is, obviously, the fundamentals – and that is best learned from a pro to reinforce book learning, humma, humma, humma, etc. Practice the delivery in the mirror, if it helps, in fact, buy a package for yourself to show how serious you are, and you can work on your own game at the same time.

Seriously, what *does* this development process that Hogan went through mean for the average player trying to improve? For one thing, nobody should finish *Five Lessons* believing that Hogan did not put everything he knew about building a powerful repeating swing "in there." I know I struggled a bit with that issue at some points in trying to work the fundamental movements into my swing, having gone from a perfectly useless slice to an increasingly uncontrollable hook.

I initially believed the story that there was something mystical Hogan did not share with "us" that was preventing my getting "it." But I had simply failed to get the fundamentals buttoned down properly and I did not believe my own eyes (I *always* thought Hogan was hitting a hook, although everyone seemingly knew better and they all told me I was seeing things) or impressions of his swing. It matters little, ATBE, where you get those fundamentals from. Think in terms of a system of fundamentals, rather than pieces and parts that are all supposed to come together to make a chicken. It should not come from a friend or relative who has been golfing for some time and "already breaks 100." Go to a local pro who can become familiar with your golf swing, tendencies, and attributes. Based on the pro assessment, you can learn how to fine tune things as necessary to suit your athletic ability. You can go back and see the pro when you need to, and the threat of proximity will work to keep you both honest.

The hand, forearm, and wrist strength necessary to play golf, but especially to swing in the manner advocated by Hogan, does not come from answering the telephone, attending meetings, or pounding the keyboard, but from pounding golf balls! I recommend *Five Lessons* as a review point or as a starting point for any golfer, without reservation, not just for beginners. I don't think there is a better description, in a clearer manner, than this timeless book. But it is unrealistic to expect to learn the game without making some type of commitment to practice, and yes, hitting balls on the range.

Are you a "technolosos" – the type of person who likes to think about angles, positions, precision, alignment, congruence, centrifugal force, supination, etc.? Do you want to know exactly what to do to hit the golf ball? An easy way to tell is to gauge your impressions of my descriptions in the book about positions, analogies, and the like. When you read below about "supination interruptess," do you start to get a little queasy and irate and want to put the book down? Or are you a "feeliosos" (I made both these words up) – the type of person who knows there are numbers involved at some level, but is not looking for anything more than the keys and a point toward the direction of travel? Or are you a little of both when it comes to things you learn in sports or athletics? Do you prefer to learn the technical so you can integrate it as you go, not dogmatic to either the technical or the feel approach, in order that when you personalize it you know when you make trades, compromises, or modifications? This last or hybrid (hybridosos?) approach is best for those who come to the game from the standpoint of learning a lifetime sport, rather than those playing a one-time scramble or a special event with the boss to be played and soon forgotten.

There are enough golf books to go around and a quick visit to a larger bookstore can resolve the issue of which text is best for you in consideration of your learning proclivity. The back of this book is by no means inclusive, but has a pretty good list.

Two things I offer while I am touching on topics that tend toward preachiness: just because we are in the twenty-first century and it is okay for people to wear fewer and smaller clothing items to the beach or the pool does not mean that everyone should partake of this freedom of expression. There is nothing mandatory or obligatory about it, if you get my drift!

What does this have to do with golf? The most important aspect of golf is golf etiquette: what you do and the manner in which you conduct yourself at the golf course. You can play lousy golf and hit horrible shots, but if you maintain your pace of play, stay pleasant, and don't ruin everyone's day with your terrible play and more so your attitude, you will be invited back. If you are the type of person who does not mind making a total embarrassment out of yourself in public and being a burden on those around you, then you can best do that somewhere other than the golf course. As a new golfer, you should be as reticent to play golf on a course with other humans in public as you would be to sing in front of an audience for the first time, or drive a motorcycle on a busy highway for the first time, or do your first public-speaking event, or run your first marathon. You are not the type of person who would seriously consider doing any of these without some type of practice, are you? You should treat golf the same way, regardless of what your twenty-six-plus index brother-in-law Numchuks tells you. It is probably not okay to just trot out to the golf course, blissfully ignorant of the conventions and rules of the game and the play. There is a myth about country-club stuffiness and "tight-cheeked" people who feel like only those with bloodlines and class should be allowed on the golf course. That is not the issue at all; the issue is really the inordinate amount of time it takes to play a round of golf, and the fact that people who don't know the rules and the conventions exacerbate it considerably.

The only thing worse than being held up or slowed down on the golf course by people who are ignorant of the basic tenets of golfing etiquette is, well, nothing; only slow play itself is worse. You can be called on it if you are holding up others and you have terrain in front of you that should be filled with golfers. Golfers should endeavor to keep pace with the players ahead of them, in fact, your job is to keep them mindful of their pace in order for them to be able to press the players ahead of them and so on. If you do fall back from the group in front of you and start to see players behind glaring like bulls set for the run of the bulls, or with hands on hips, you should either let people play through, pick up your ball and go to the next hole, or make some other similar adjustment to get caught up to the group in front of you. A round of golf should never, ever, take more than four hours, and play with carts should be much less. There is nothing wrong with taking your time on the range, in the pro shop, the nineteenth hole; enjoying the day, smelling the flowers, enjoying the views. But when you get out on the course, convention dictates that one should move out as if one has a purpose, as they say, with somewhat of a sense of urgency and do your talking, scoring, tips, drips, and jokes in the cart (while it is moving.)

We play ready golf, which means whoever is ready to play, plays, and if someone in our foursome gets crazy and is taking their time lining up a putt for a triple or quadruple bogey, we tell them to "pick it up" or "that's good." Saving a little bit of time in this manner can go a long way to keeping our group on pace with the group ahead of us and to ensure we are not ruining someone else's day by playing slowly. That someone else is you. You are probably like me; we never play slow, it's always someone else causing the problem. Remember that someone else and ensure that it's not you. And I will watch me!

Many a summer has gone by without playing much golf because I could not commit to the five or six hours it was going to take to play a round. It's inexcusable that golf in the U.S. takes so long to play. A big contributor to that phenomenon is the delusion that it is a fundamental right of all, having paid their green fee, to be able to just trot out and play without knowing anything about the sport. The elimination of the five- or six-hour round should be a goal of every golfing enterprise and every golfer in the U.S.

It's unfortunate that common sense ain't so common these days, but you can help by contributing to the growing list of people who are righteously indignant that golf on the weekend is taking longer and longer to complete, while handicaps are not improving from year to year. A friend of mine committed to getting better by adopting many of the habits he observed on television by those terrible examples, the touring professionals. What a joy to experience and behold! He would take as many practice swings as necessary until he *felt* the right swing for the shot he was playing. When it was his turn to putt, rather than taking care of some of his business while others were putting, he would start his procedure at that point, much like he practiced it, plumb-bobbing and lining it up from both sides, taking a peek in the cup at the pattern of grass to discern the break and taking as many practice strokes as needed until it *felt* right. The last several times I played with him, everyone in the foursome unconsciously started to rush to make up for his slow play. Such behavior totally extrudes the fun out of the round. On many of the military courses, you only get one or two chances to do the right thing, e.g., speed it up or let somebody through, before someone is either in your face or golf balls are raining down upon you. More extrusion of fun! My friend had unfortunately ingrained this procedure through practice, if you can imagine, and he felt like we were trying to *rush him* when we talked about some of the ready golf tenets that applied to the green, as well.

Having a good pre-shot routine and repeating a consistent routine for hitting the ball is important in the final analysis, but these are not substitutes for a sound technique, a good swing or for common sense in your approach to your play. Put a bit differently, no amount of routine is going to make up for bad technique; a nineteen handicap is only going to improve so much with a better routine, all things being equal. Hiding behind dark glasses can only do so much for you at the pool or the beach. And you already know the deal with the lipstick and the pig.

There is no substitute for professional guidance and practice. Much like learning anything new, some type of happy compromise should be reached between your playing and practicing. I have no special insights to offer in that regard other than my own nearly two decades of ball beating. But if you have several hours to spend, hit some practice balls and play nine holes. If you have an hour and a half, hit some practice balls, chip, and putt. If you have a half-day, hit some practice shots and play some golf. If your handicap is really high (above average) and you have been playing for awhile, ATBE, take a walk and enjoy the day and spend some money and time getting lessons. Golf is enjoyable no matter what, but I don't understand how anyone can enjoy playing golf while shooting scores that high and not doing something about it, ATBE (and I mean health, limbs, faculties, etc.).

I went the better part of my life with little to no time or desire to improve my golf. I enjoyed playing but as I mention elsewhere, I did not consider it a sport like hockey, tennis, baseball, or Tae Kwon Do, and I have never been able to play if I have anything pending. Two experiences drove me to improve my golf. One relates to when I started to learn about it in 1991 and one applies to my recent efforts from 2006 to the present.

I played quite a bit of tennis growing up, but really did not know much about the sport from a technical standpoint. When I joined the Army and was stationed in Colorado, playing at altitude at Fort Carson, Colorado, in the thin air at 5600 feet was significantly different than the sea level, heavy air, high-humidity largely baseline-style tennis game I grew up playing in Cranston, Rhode Island.

Rushing the net, serve and volley-style tennis was the norm in Colorado, rather than the baseline game I grew up with. I decided to try to learn that aspect of the game. What a shock it was for me to discover that there was an entire science and discipline behind many of the aspects of the game I already played, and in particular, to those aspects differentiating slow from fast court techniques! I played for all those years blissfully ignorant of much of the technique, terminology, and corresponding strategy. The learning experience I went through paved the way for my later investigation into golf.

The other learning experience was music. I had long played basic chords on the guitar, but never had much time to learn to play, so I pretty much focused on the open chords in the first position, playing popular songs that I liked. My brothers both play very well, in fact, each had taken up the guitar when we were kids and kept it up over the years. When we played together on infrequent occasions, I usually put the guitar away for several months afterward as the experience reinforced for me that I knew nothing about playing guitar and I had no time to learn. But I inevitably started playing again each time, because I enjoyed playing. I finally resolved after my last session with them in 2003 that I either had to quit once and for all, or learn more. I had no concept of the structure or makeup of the musical ideas they were referring to from even the most basic sense of the word. I had purchased an acoustic guitar in 1978 and played it off and on since then, so we are really talking about the "slow and the intellectually incurious" in my case.

The guitar purchase is applicable to golf, as you will see. I was looking to spend fifty or sixty dollars on a "cheapie." The salesman asked what I was looking for in a guitar. When I explained I was a beginner, just looking for something cheap, he asked me if I played any other sports. I said tennis, and he asked what type of racquet I played with and how much I routinely spent for them. When I told him seventy-five to a hundred dollars, he asked why I didn't buy the cheaper racquets that were available. I answered that they wouldn't last, they were inferior, etc. He told me I was looking at ten-dollar racquets. That resonated as a big touché for me. So I bought a decent guitar that I have to this day. That is a good story to think about the next time you are eyeing value-priced golf clubs in Zipmart or the bargain store.

I started taking music lessons in 2003. The lessons resulted in several aha moments as I learned about the fret board. I was somewhat chagrined and rueful thinking about the long time I had gone without doing what would have been a fairly easy thing to do, namely, take lessons, and the amount of time I wasted in the sessions with my brothers over the years. As I observed earlier, nothing is obvious to the uninformed. But analogous to golf, I bought lesson books or music-instruction books over the years, only to discover that, much like golf, instructors often used a different verbiage, lexicon, and approach to the descriptions, which did not foster interest or learning, at least for what I was looking to assimilate.

Eventually I learned the meaning of "chromatic" and I became convinced that there must be a systematic way to find the open chords throughout the neck. I now understood that things started repeating at the twelfth fret, but I also needed to solidify the implications in my mind. It was purely by digging through the available instructional literature (and much like golf, there are scads of references) that I stumbled onto Bill Edwards wonderful instruction books called *Fretboard Logic*. This series not only perfectly suited my learning temperament, but he provided an aha moment in describing the "CAGED" sequence to chords that could have saved me a lot of time and trouble these past thirty years.

His intro to the section "The Caged Sequence-Chords" starts with the following admonition: "If you've never seen this before, by the time you finish this section, you'll understand why the author considers the inventor of the guitar's tuning system among the unsung heroes in music history." He then provides the structured system that can be applied to find the basic chord sequences throughout the neck.

What is the relative importance of the above to the topic at hand? Nothing is obvious to the uninformed! When I played with my brothers the next summer, I was somewhat surprised that the *Fretboard Logic* insights were not as well known as I thought (and that I was not as late to the party as I believed!), although much of the focus of the book they had worked through intuitively during their own three-decade or so experience. Separately, my efforts over the past several years have resulted in a better appreciation for the dedication it takes to become good at things like music or golf, where a combination of knowledge, desire, and talent combine to produce results. My instructor, Matthew Mills, was voted by *GuitarWorld* (July 2008) as eighteenth out of the top-fifty fastest guitar players of all time, based on an assessment of published or recorded music, and the fact that he played fourteen notes per second. The skill he has achieved through practice is astounding and not unlike the path to perfection that led Hogan to achieve his goals so many years ago. Matt's staggering talent can be viewed on the Internet and I will tell you it is real and not sped up!

This is offered to reinforce the importance of getting good help or focused instruction, and for that you should see a pro. You can start your effort at the most advanced level possible, ATBE, given your aptitude, attitude, athletic ability, and capacity for practice. I think this was part of Hogan's lament in *Five Lessons* about how long he had been in golf.

I offer these explanations because I can appreciate that it is easy to say, "Just go practice," for someone who enjoys hitting practice balls. But what if you are the Jack Nicklaus type, who only needs to hit golf balls when he is working on something? Who can simply walk away from the rest of the pile when he reaches his objective, whether it's the tenth or fiftieth ball? I guess I am either thrifty (okay, cheap) or simple, but even when I complete what I want to do, I feel obligated to hit the rest of the balls I have. But did we just compare you to Jack Nicklaus? That would put you in the lowest-possible percentile of golfers who have plus indexes and who break par each time they play. Probably not a relevant comparison, but how much time would it take for someone with average skills to pick up the basic moves and learn to play golf? Well, it takes twenty-one days just to ingrain new habits. The trial-and-error method just takes too long and fails to foster an increasingly important aspect, namely, confidence. The only worse impediment to improvement than poor fundamentals is the development of a storehouse of bad-shot memories. Good instruction is the way to go.

In cases like my own where I felt like my action was already similar to that described in *Five Lessons*, I believe it helps with the development of each facet of the game to build pieces within a system. The earlier reference to David Leadbetter's instruction is equally germane, as I worked through the positions in his books "by the numbers" to good effect before I realized that, while I learn better with mechanics, I play better focusing on shots. It is difficult to do the one if you are intent on implementing the other (at least for me). But his book, much like Hogan's *Five Lessons*, breaks it down into manageable chunks and small pieces. I think the series is especially good for taller players wrestling with stability and lower-body issues.

There are dozens of very good books on the market. As an aside, the Faldo you will meet on the Leadbetter tapes, should you go that route, bears no resemblance to the chap the writers have been bashing all these years. Long before he became "human" through broadcasting golf in the U.S., the tapes provided a startling contrast to his public image – kind of like someone else we have been discussing, *n'est ce pas?*

The real problem with trial and error is the lack of feedback to prevent ingraining bad habits, and also the time it takes to work through the fundamentals. Video can help if you can analyze it in an unbiased way, which can be hard. The time spent getting the fundamentals correct is a down payment on the future, whereas doing it wrong is an investment in a future reclamation project. In my own case, I sliced for a long time after I weakened my grip a bit. This was due to a number of reasons, but chiefly from a poor but aggressive weight shift, a wandering right elbow, and a faulty concept of impact. I videotaped my swing and I was clearly swinging down too much, coming over the top, and getting toe-bound with my weight. Seeing faults is one thing; I had no idea what to do about it, and it took a long time before I figured out the true cause and applied the correct fixes. That time would have been better spent taking lessons from a pro, rather than grooving the compensations to the faults and making them part of my swing, where I later had to unlearn them. However, a revamping of my swing would probably have precluded me getting to this book!

Take a relatively simple fundamental concept like the plane, which Hogan described as increasingly important to him as he integrated his swing. I did not really integrate the plane as an element to be concerned about until the last several years. If you try to hit a fade and make a very natural move that results in a lifting of the arms and a pronounced movement from outside to inside, you are toast as far as consistency. A lousy shot will generally result. Why? *Supination interuptus*! Because it causes your plane to go upright (or downright) and it really narrows the "okay" window for the hands coming into the hitting zone, bringing the clubhead back to the ball with the hands out of position or oriented in the wrong position. What exactly does that mean? For technolosos, that means that as the knees flex and the hips turn and produce torque that ripples up the sides of your chest to the shoulders, the inside upper arm and shoulder adhesion to the chest starts to generate inside or centripetal pulling power that is transmitted via the upper arms, elbows, and forearms to the hands, in turn. The rotary inside pressure eventually causes the lead hand to be pulled toward impact like the end of the whip, trailing, lagging or simply behind all the other parts and producing that magical supination move or the bow of the wrist forward through the ball (it always struck me that to say it bows forward is somewhat misleading, as it is clearly the trailing or lagging left side element. The position is more akin to a flipper midway through a power stroke. Bowed back makes more sense, but the normal reference is used here for consistency.) Squaring the clubface through and past impact with speed depends or relies on the hands being in the correct position and naturally, also (because they are connected) the clubface; so being in a bad position inhibits proper release. What does that mean? You have a hitch in your giddy-up! You are *catawampus*, as a colleague would say, unable to get your gait straight and trot!

Assuming I haven't lost anyone, but for feeliosos especially, the feeling you want through impact is the feeling you have when you are participating in a tug of war; you lean back with all your might (you are pulling the rope from behind you or to your right, facing toward the direction of pull) and gather and grab the rope and pull—and it is like you are a giant; the rope just comes with ease. *Supination interruptus* is the opposite feeling; you have braced yourself and gathered the rope and pulled but you are facing a bigger giant and you are stuck partway through a power or supination stroke, unable to complete the power cycle. *Supination interuptus*! For hybridosos, you firmly grab the car door and start to shut it when it recoils off the seatbelt hanging out of the car before you manage to pull your hand away. Even simpler, you lean back to cast your fishing rod but it gets caught in something and you get stuck halfway through the cast.

CHAPTER TEN

Getting the Feel of "It" Exemplars. Are You a Technolosos or a Feeliosos?

"Nothing is obvious to the uninformed."
Carry Morgan

We have already accrued a potentially ruinous number of assumptions here, assuming a good grip, stance, posture, etc. I'm also assuming the use of inside muscles, as Hogan recommends. I used the outside muscles for years with weight shifted forward of center and a bad action that fostered varying degrees of wicked slices, and never really felt a natural release through the ball until I puzzled over the terms in *Five Lessons*. I mention elsewhere in the book about improving my golf on the Bayonet Golf Course, Fort Ord, California. I never much worried about my slice in Arizona, as I hit it pretty good; and when I blocked it right, it generally went far enough right that I usually found a fairway. Bayonet is lined with trees. My handicap became much worse before it got much better, since although it is not quite a Cardinal Rule, suffice it to say, it is hard playing good golf out of trees.

Much complication over nothing you say (you technolosos or feeliosos, you?), how much work will you commit to and what does it take to ingrain the correct feeling in order to translate and reproduce it in your golf swing? Here are a couple of easy drills to feel some of the correct positions (right now).

Just stand naturally in a loose golf-type stance and balance your weight on your right leg by lifting your left foot to the toe and, for as long as you can, off the ground, to help you get the feel of the weight inside the leg, vice outside, but settling back to where the left toe is the only contact point for the left side. Do the same with the left side, lifting the right foot until only the very tip of the toe is on the ground. The point of this is to feel the balance point "inside" the supporting leg and it is the way the swing should move, from inside to inside, and feel, all things being equal. The less comfortable you are initially, the more to the inside the body needs to lean to compensate to maintain balance.

Here is another variation of the drill. Stand naturally and raise the heel of your left foot so the preponderance or bulk of the weight shifts to your right side. Do not raise or lower your body or your head during the transition; both should be "quiet." Now do the opposite, raising your right heel as your left settles down. Vary it a bit and exaggerate the movement until you start dramatically shifting your weight (which remains on the inside of the leg in either case, right or left), then back it off again so you feel like there is just a minor shift, but felt more like leverage or a cantilever-type action.

This simple drill extended into the movement described as the hip-to-hip drill (or a half-swing back and a half-swing forth on page 82) in *Five Lessons* is all you need, provided your fundamentals are sound, to learn the knockdown swing. The knockdown swing is a partial swing described earlier that has a lower trajectory and about three-fourths the distance of the club being hit. Need more detail? Place your arms tightly against your sides or upper chest and place your hands in a position like you are holding a club (but don't for now.) Rise up on your left heel and turn your upper body clockwise or to the right until your left arm is at the nine o'clock position described earlier. To be a bit persnickety about it, your shoulder should have turned about ninety degrees or so; your arms should remain adhered tightly (emphasize the point) to the side of your chest and your hands should feel or look like you are holding a baseball bat in the ready position, and your weight should feel inside. Your hips only turn to the degree pulled by the shoulders. Now simply drop your left heel and raise your right heel, not rushing through the transition of the weight transfer from one leg or one side to the other. The minimal tension you feel that makes your shoulders move, that tugs your arm and puts pressure on your hands is the free ride that Hogan refers to in *Five*

Lessons.

If you do this with attention to detail, adding in a linebacker-ready position or golf-address posture, adding some pressure or tension to the upper arms, slamming those heels down to stress and torque the pieces, over-adhering the arms to the body, you will feel how the arms move without conscious thought, but also how those recalcitrant limbs want to naturally do the wrong things. Just when the body has put you in a perfect position to hit, centrifugal force causes the arms and hands to want to wander to the outside and to take over and add power in a manner that is ruinous! This is the over-the-top move that ruins more swings than rust and bad weather! This is one thing Hogan meant about doing the opposite of the natural tendency of the body. And not to complicate things, but the force you want to feel to engender the use, sensation, and feel of the inside muscles is centripetal, vice centrifugal force, at least as far as Hogan's methodology is concerned, whereby you optimize supination. Rather than thinking about holding a club for this drill, think about the way you would pull that rope. You can't push it, it is like a noodle. You can't fling it, it is too long and it isn't in the proper position to be flung yet. And you can't flick it; it is not in position to do any of these things yet. The only option you have is to deliberately pull that rope kind of horizontally downward by focusing on the pulling sensation building at the inside of the left bicep caused by adhesion and the rotation initially of the left chest and the fulcrum-like pressure that big muscle is exerting on its little brethren (assuming you are right-handed.) A picture sequence would be easier to digest, but this relatively simple drill can be done right here, right now as you read and it is indicative of the problems Hogan alluded to when he talked about doing the opposite of what the body wants to do (the opposite of the natural tendency).

I think it is instructive to address one of those ruinous tendencies now, so you know what to look out for in your own trials. Once you lower the left heel and raise the right, and your shoulder starts to follow the hip and chest around and the pressure causes downward force as the shoulders start to unwind, moving the arms forward and making them want to sling out naturally from the body, straighten the right arm as fast as you can. This is the best way to foul up everything you have just gotten in position to do properly. That is a false power move that is simply ruinous. Most slicers instinctively execute this movement.

This is not the position Hogan was talking about getting to so he could apply power, as much as three right hands, because "he would know what to do with it." That position has not been reached yet. The position reached with our drill is getting to the "slot," or delivery position, the prelude to the box or impact sequence. From this point forward, it is "safe" to observe any of the aforementioned distinctive swings, like "Mr. X" Miller Barber and Jim Furyk.

To feel the position Hogan was talking about, get back to the nine o'clock position with your left heel raised; now lower your left heel and raise your right heel. As you feel the pressure or power building in your left shoulder, let your arms move naturally and envision that you have a device that has the golf ball on a tall tee like the type kids use for tee-ball. As your arms move, driven by the big muscles of the chest, linked to the movement dictated by the transfer of weight and the pressure built through adhesion, you simply want to stab that ball with the butt end of your hand (the grip) as hard as you can do it without giving a thought to using the hands. That is very close to the position Hogan was talking about (and in a perfect position to shank). What is the actual position? Do the same drill I just described, only this time, hit the ball as hard as you can with the back of your left hand. When you do it correctly, everything should be ahead of the back of the hand or, conversely, the back of the hand should be losing the race with the left side to get to impact. If it hesitates at all it will be overrun by the right side, starting with the right hand. Hold the contact position and look at the right hand. It should be in a position like you are shaking hands with someone who is somewhat "downstairs" from you, palm open facing relative to the ball, still relatively "cupped" or pronated in its own "right," somewhat down or canted/shaded closed, and not as yet unleashed by the left hand/left side at this point. The elbow is still against the body and the upper right arm is about to propel the forearm and hand inside and through, coming off the torque being transferred from the left side to the hips and to the upper body.

This is the shortstop throw to first-base sidearm position from *Five Lessons*. The one piece I omitted or failed to place in its proper place is the slightly "squatty" look and feel the body transitions through as the weight shifts forward into (or onto) the inside left side. The step of the shortstop initiates that "squatty" look and feel. I also like the analogy of getting in position to close a really heavy gate, fast, with the right hand on the gate. The other feeling that comes to mind, particularly for the forward part of the swing, is you should have the feel of a hammer-thrower or someone struggling to throw a keg. The correct position of the hands is depicted in many books such as *Five Lessons*, but quite simply make a fist and you will see that your hand knows what to do to get in the proper position with regard to the arm. And the best thing for you to do is to stay out of the process! The proper movement of the right arm and hand is important, and I did not get it clear in my own head until I read somewhere or heard someone discuss (Johnny Miller, *Pure Golf?*) how the right palm tries to work "downward," or facing the ground, through impact, in a painting or washing (swishing) type of motion. It is unable to do so because the left hand won't breakdown enough to allow it to and the hands are at the end of the arms, so they get pulled leftward as they bump at the bottom of the arc of the plane, but that is the feel of the motion described. The only reason the right hand is allowed to move downward at all is that the slinging effect, e.g., supination (of the left hand) forces it to, but with the bump against the bottom of the arc, it never makes it. I would have bet money at one time that the proper motion of the right hand was up and sideward! There are no secrets to these positions; the technique is allowing the sequence to unfold naturally as an element of your swing, and to adjust your aim point to accommodate the results. These natural moves are moves that can easily be repeated whether you are sharp or "have it or not" (hint, hint) that morning.

With the kind indulgence of the feeliosos, we technolosos can clarify a few more things of importance. I did not mention rolling the club face, pronation, or the deliberate manipulation of any of the positions described above. The body produces these moves as part of the chain action established by moving through the proper positions. I stress the point about supination because it is a natural move that is rarely achieved by most golfers since they are busy pouring on the power, which breaks down the left hand, or makes it impossible for the hands to function properly. Golfers most often rush through the supination phase of the swing because the body and brain signal that the slight pause, indicating the hands are getting ready to transfer power through the ball, is translated as a natural urge or feeling that the swing is falling behind and must be rushed to catch-up, thereby ruining the chain action and eliminating any chance of feeling the "sling" of a proper golf swing. It is essential to have a clear sense of what the body, but more importantly the arm-club line, looks like at impact. This is the move that ties all the good golfers together, including "Mr. X" and Jim Furyk, and I suggest, keeps bad golfers from improving their handicaps.

Your swing plane will produce a bad result if the backswing line you have chosen is markedly above or below the relative position to the orientation or angle formed as measured from the center point of your turning shoulder axis or pivot point, extrapolated through the ball to form the center line of the approach. A simpler and more elegant description of the previous is that you must stay below the plane of glass (*Five Lessons*). Swinging the club back markedly above or below the glass (as evidenced by the forearms losing contact or breaking the glass) will cause the hands to miss the available margin of error in relation to the window, or aperture, they must pass through to supinate properly prior to impact. And it would be easy enough to calculate a margin of error with a robot or "Iron Byron" type of swing device. A simple way to keep it in mind during the swing is to pre-stage the path via the waggle, which is one of the genius techniques Hogan integrated within his swing. I believe there is no set correct plane for every golfer. A friend of mine is a good-sized human being, about six feet, four inches, and about 290 pounds. I was shocked when I put on the wrong jeans one day, where the waist was big enough for three of me, but the pants were too short! And I have longer arms proportionally, than most people of my height, so his shirts are just about the right sleeve length, although the twenty-one-inch neck was a bit much. But there is no possibility that the same plane would be correct for both of us.

Regarding the swing and impact, a good visual to think about is the hinged lever described in *The Search for the Perfect Swing*. The arms do not achieve a relatively straight line until just after impact, which is the only time in the swing that both arms are straight. Repeat that to yourself a dozen times or more. There is no rush to straighten the arms during your swing, in fact, the longer you can delay the straightening, all things being equal, the more crisply you will hit your irons. The feeling or impression that you are behind somehow, or that you can't quite get in the proper position to hit, or that something is lagging or late, that is the late hit or supination feeling through impact. The natural tendency to fix and correct the feeling of lateness or of being behind must be beaten into submission through practice. That is the body trying to do what feels right by messing up your swing.

The visual and feel are extremely important to capturing the essence of the details. A clear example that captures the swing plane, the margin of error, and supination is the one outlined above, but easier to grasp is to think about splashing water in a pool. You can swing your palm with as much force as you can generate, but if it is oriented to the water improperly, no splash will result. If you attempt to splash with the back of your hand you will wrestle with a simple form of supination akin to the golf swing release. Think of how complicated it would be to explain in myriad detail how to properly splash someone, whereas an average person can learn to splash in the pool within two minutes. Similarly, think of other things you accomplish, such as writing with a pencil, turning on a light switch, or similar routine functions, where you never give a second thought to things such as grip, grip pressure, angles, etc.

Put your feet together and hold a club. Move the club back to where the left arm is parallel to the ground and the right elbow is closely tucked to the side. It feels and looks like a baseball player holding a bat at the ready and it is the base position for the knockdown swing. Now step sideways with your left foot about shoulder width or more apart, which moves the bulk of your weight to the *inside* of your left side, and simply let your arms go with the natural tendency to follow down and through the ball. If done properly, using the inside muscles, keyed off the pressure caused by the chest on the left arm and adhesion of the right arm and elbow to the side, the predominant feeling is not a hit or a chop, but the beginning of a sling. Yes, a sling or a fling. Tom Bertrand in his book *The Secret of Hogan's Swing* relates how John Shlee used a drill in his school where he had the students "fling" or sling golf clubs by letting them go toward a target. This is a great drill to ingrain the feel of what I just described, although most golfers will have not experienced anything like it before! So it is very difficult, if done properly without emphasis on the hands (de-emphasizing the hands), to close the clubface before impact. You have to manipulate something abnormally to achieve a closed clubface before impact if you only concentrate on the arms. You should have a sense that you are trying to straighten out your right forearm at the ball, but are unable to do it. You don't want to do it, all things being equal! That feeling of not quite getting the club or swing to the point where you think it should be is the much-touted late hit, lag, X-factor or delayed hit that Hogan made so famous.

Hogan's drill for hip-to-hip contact from a feet parallel position is a great one for the arms and body synchronization feel. The value of this drill is that when it is done properly, it takes the hands out of consideration as a point of emphasis because any focus on the hands to the exclusion of the arms will wreck the timing. If you did nothing more than perfect this drill to the point where you could reproduce on demand the action of the arms, you would improve immensely. This is also the key sequence to learning the knockdown swing.

As I mentioned earlier, a knockdown swing is a partial swing that hits the ball pretty much straight along the intended line at around seventy-five percent of the normal club distance, necessitating about two less clubs for an equivalent shot. The best way to feel the proper sequence for the drill might be to do it badly several times as a contrast to the correct sequence of movements (everyone learns differently.) To do the anti-drill, as the weight shifts, let it go to the outside of your left leg, which constitutes a slide that breaks the synchronization of the left and right sides. Now straighten the right arm as fast as you can so it moves away from your hip. You will probably block it out to a two o'clock position or smother it with a dead pull to the left. If you occasionally hit it properly doing this drill as described, then congratulations, you have just discovered a ruinous compensation move that has been unconsciously ingrained in your swing as an exemplar that you have come to believe is "close to correct." It's not! Don't strive to reproduce the forty-sixty percent of the time you get lucky and all the compensations produce a good shot. Fix the forty-sixty percent of the time when contact is not quite satisfactory, by doing the opposite of your natural tendency.

A reasonable athlete with good fundamentals should be able to produce a satisfactory knockdown shot from this drill and hit a much higher proportion of good shots with perhaps several practice sessions of ten-to-twenty attempts. Just because it is a partial swing does not mean you slow anything down or do anything markedly different than a normal swing. The arms must swing every bit as fast as the demands placed upon them by the body dictate. The easiest way to bollix up this drill is by disconnecting the arms somehow, thinking it's a partial swing so they don't need to keep pace, or by overachieving, so rather than getting seventy-five percent of the normal club distance, you strive for eighty or ninety percent. Trust me on this one; even if you are special and you turn out to be the only human in the world who can get more than seventy-five percent out of this shot without over swinging or losing consistency, keep it to yourself. It will be your little edge; but in the meantime, work on the seventy-five percent figure. There are no points rewarded for anything that happens before the ball settles in the cup; and much like baseball, your scorecard does not reflect how you did it, but what you scored.

About the only way to achieve this "improper drill" is to stop or quit with the left side, and if you get your left side too far ahead it will be impossible to swing through properly, anyway; you will definitely feel a hitch in your giddy up! Either way you achieve disastrous results. Doing it wrong feels like you have a giant dart in your arms that you are trying to stick in the ground as deep as you can, rather than having the feeling of flinging the giant dart horizontally to your left. The correct motion should remind you of throwing a Frisbee, or slinging that long gate closed, or dragging a heavy duffle bag out from behind you that you fear will get caught on the outside of your right leg, so you are pulling it, in effect, around you by swinging out and around but with a respectful fear not to swing out and around too much. The right side stays pretty much behind the ball prior to impact.

In some cases excessive detail is not much help without a sense of the larger concept, in other cases it's a big help in general, and in still others a lack of detail is ruinous. Much like Hogan said and insinuated in *Five Lessons*, things that are done with the hope of improving your golf must be pretty close to perfectly executed to enable the next step, and the next step, to unfold correctly. Being almost right in these cases can be an impediment to progress. The reason Hogan specifically addresses the issue of detail and the fact that he could sometimes be, well, persnickety, is that being close to doing it right is not going to cut it. For instance, if you disregard the admonition about the plane and opt for a more upright plane than recommended because many feel it is a key to longer distance, you are going to struggle mightily with supination, and you will not get the crisp iron contact (consistently) that produces natural spin on the ball. But you may be lucky (or unlucky) enough to combine the faults just right a sufficient number of times to delude yourself into believing you are close to mastering the technique. You can spend a lifetime of golf seasons right around the corner from mastery.

I don't have much to say about that old bugaboo, distance, as I think it is the most common-sense piece of the game. How did someone like Ben Hogan, at five feet, eight inches, and 140 pounds, hit the ball three hundred yards with the low technology equipment available in the day? Solid fundamentals, swing speed, and solid contact. There is no magic to be applied. How fast can you swing the club, do you know? A friend of mine grew tired of adding new drivers to his bag every year after they increased in price to more than four hundred dollars each. He finally asked me how it was that I out-drove him with my old technology and my crappy flat swing. I asked him what his swing speed was, and his reply was, "I have no idea." I told him I probably averaged a bit over 112 miles per hour (mph) or so with the driver, and he was below one hundred – and that was the main difference. He didn't believe that there could be that much a difference; he was stronger, bigger, had better swing fundamentals. He called me out of the blue one day and we went to Washington Golf Center over lunchtime one afternoon. I was in a suit; he was in an exercise outfit with sneakers. We quickly discovered that his warm up swings were below ninety mph and if he swung as hard as he could to the point where he thought he was going to blow a hamstring, he swung ninety-eight mph with the driver, and his best was 103 mph. He was sweating profusely at the exertion (I grew weary watching him) but he was getting the point.

  I had not planned to swing since I was in a suit, but you know how these things go at times. Between my friend insisting that there was no way I swung as fast as I said, and the "expert" working the place telling me that the pros only swung about 110 mph maximum, and that I was not big enough to swing faster than that since it's a combination of height and strength, etc., etc. So, my warm-up swings were around 105 mph and what felt like my eighty-five percent swing was 114 mph, which was a bit more than I remembered (attributable, no doubt, to the new driver technology.) When I turned it up a notch and felt like I was swinging hard, I was consistently over 115 and I started to lose square contact at that point. Swing speed is an important element to use for a number of things related to your game, including equipment and shaft issues but not the least of which is distance calculations. I had checked my swing speed out years before and now my friend knows his as well. I resolved to check out the new technology if I get playing more frequently in the future! Hogan achieved his impressive distance through swing speed and solid contact. For him to hit the golf balls of his day close to three hundred yards with persimmon woods and steel shafts means he was swinging the golf club over 120 miles per hour!

  If you are looking for more distance (and who isn't?), fix your fundamentals and swing a weighted club to build up the proper muscles. The faster you can get your eighty-five percentage or normal swing, the longer you will hit the ball given solid contact. The faster you try to swing, the less solid your contact will be (ATBE) and the less distance you will hit it. It's that simple. It is very important as you get better to know how far you carry your shots in the air, and how far you hit each club. There is not much point in learning a knockdown shot that you can hit solidly anytime, even when under severe choking conditions, if you don't know the number to apply to derive the seventy-five percent of the equation. You could do it the other way, that is, work the knockdown with each club in the bag and derive your normal distances. Endeavor to work on increasing your distance through sound fundamentals, solid contact, and increasing your capability to swing the club faster (not harder). The measure is swing speed. Get to know your distances.

There are many good books available about the short game so I will use less detail on this topic. The more you play, the better your short game will get. I know a lot of people who have settled for less-than-optimal basic golf games because of the strength of their short games. They can get the ball up and down from just about anywhere and they can be a huge source of frustration for golfers who misjudge their non-classical games. Just because you don't hit a lot of fairways and greens does not mean you can't post good scores. The scorecard doesn't know and does not care. A classic case in point: Tiger Woods. At times his ball striking has approached that of a ten handicap, but his uncanny ability to get the ball up and down makes his scorecard look like he is the greatest golfer in the world (which he obviously is)!

Around 1991 I adopted Paul Runyon's methodology outlined in *The Short Way to Lower Scoring*. Runyon is among the greatest players and instructors in the history of the game. Talk about challenged, he was diminutive in comparison to Hogan, if you can imagine, and he never averaged more than about 230 yards or so off the tee in his career during the 1930s and '40s. So he routinely gave up ten to fifteen yards to the light hitters (e.g. Cooper and Guldahl), never mind the twenty-five to thirty yards he gave up to medium hitters (e.g. Nelson and Little). With the bigger hitters such as Craig Wood and Horton Smith, he gave up thirty-five yards or more, and with the longer hitters like Thompson, Hebert, Hogan or Snead, he gave up an average of forty yards off the tee. But his adept short game allowed him to keep up with and beat those better-known golfers in their prime. He won twenty-four tournaments on tour, including two PGA Championships, and was the leading money winner in 1933-34 and 1937-38. His 1938 PGA Championship victory at Shawnee-On-Delaware Country Club, Pennsylvania, over Sam Snead in his prime, by eight and seven, might be the greatest upset in Championship golf since Francis Ouimet won the U.S. Open (even considering the two San Francisco debacles, Palmer failing to win with a seven-stroke lead and Jack Fleck beating Hogan in a playoff, although Hogan was forty-three years old and in extended time). Runyon beat Snead by getting the ball consistently up and down and keeping relentless pressure on Snead by being on the green first and closer on all but the par fives.

Runyon had a system for the short game and the part shots of golf. His recommendations to deal with the yips, using the split hand grip on a longer putter, were decades ahead of their time. But as he noted, the bane of his existence as a teacher was his inability to have top-flight professionals adopt his methodology. He attributed that to the pros already having good short games. You must be fairly good at the short game to get to the pro level in the first place. Pros are therefore reticent to adopt any methodology that would force them to change long-ingrained habits for a new technique that might take awhile and result in a lessening of their capability (in the short term). Translated, that means less money during the learning stage. It took me almost two years (part-time) to learn his methodology, and I use it to this day. So, there is help available in this part of the game, and you can likewise use help from a pro to develop a sound fundamental approach. If you are one of those people who has trouble with bunkers, or suffers from the yips, give Runyon's book a read. He was a master at this part of the game and you can't help learning from his book.

CHAPTER ELEVEN

Why Me? Digging It Out Of The Dirt, Too

"Hope is not a plan."
Mark Choiniere

I was an Army test officer, both military and government civilian servant, for almost seven years and I worked another five years or so in a similar capacity. I was raised an analyst as an Army enlisted image interpreter and as the officer equivalent, called the tactical surveillance officer. I studied and taught martial arts for many years, primarily Tae Kwon Do, but also Hap Kido. My black belt these days is in information analysis; many of my coworkers over the years have considered me an example of the Latin phrase, *"anal retentus extremis maximus amongus,"* or anal retentive, for short. While not normally considered a compliment, I don't mind, as I feel there is a big problem with the lack of accountability and attention to detail on most large government programs and the manner in which our tax dollars are spent. We will leave that discussion for another day.

I have come to believe that no one left on this earth, with the exception of Ken Venturi, is aware of the circumstances surrounding the development of Hogan's swing technique and the swing keys that constituted his secret. I also believe that Ken Venturi is an honorable man who made a promise not to disclose what he was told, and who feels bound by that promise to this day. Ken has simply responded during interviews that the secret was "up here or in his head," or that it was "psychological," as had Gene Sarazen also said at one point.

I literally dug the secret out of the ground through trials and tribulations with my own swing. Reading, testing, hitting thousands of golf balls over the years when I could, including lunchtime buckets, employing trial and error, putting in five a.m. sessions at local driving ranges, hitting balls back to the hitting areas – with more trial and error, study, reading, and basically digging it out of the proverbial dirt. I was not looking for a secret, per se, during the time when I was trying to improve my swing up through about 2006. Nor was I obsessed with or even thinking about a secret or any secrets or anything related to that topic. I was just trying to improve my technique and gain some consistency. Later I struggled with the puzzle about what was so hard about this confounding game and why a direct translation of the fundamentals in *Five Lessons* did not translate directly to more consistent golf for me.

Only in the last two years, as I became convinced that there was something critical missing and that it could not be in the swing at all, did I actually begin to focus on a methodology to solve the puzzle. Sometime around 2003 or so, I purchased and watched with great interest the *Hogan-Snead Wonderful World of Golf* video, in particular, the tips offered by each golfer at the end of the match. I suspected I was totally off base each time I watched Hogan swing on video; my impression over the years has been shock that he did not still have a hooking problem! I never saw a swing from him that did not look like it would produce a hook, with his powerful move onto the left side. For a time I believed I must be missing something in my analysis. Any time I mentioned that he had a strong hooking action, you would think I had accused the Pope of wearing Sponge Bob Squarepants briefs! Everyone I spoke to about it told me in nauseating detail about his fade action.

Recent releases of Hogan's swing on video during this time period helped immensely and reinforced my belief that the secret must have been in his clubs and setup, because his was a hook action if I know anything about golf at all! In fact, of all the videos I obtained over the years and the swing instruction books that have full swings, such as those produced over the years in the golf magazines, I don't remember seeing a stronger hook action through impact than Hogan's. I chalked that up to how little I knew about the fundamentals of the swing, but I always felt like the clues were there for all to see, and his action looked like he was hitting the ball to the left!

Hogan often said that if you did the exact opposite of what your body wanted to do, you might just play good golf. In hindsight, I am struck more by how deceptively simple but counter intuitive his methodology was, and, well, how "right there" it was all the time, as well as how long it took me to literally stumble upon it. The same could be said about his quest, having consumed nearly a decade and a half of his time. As I recall the sequence of events, I was looking to solidify the feeling that I was using the inside muscles of the arms and the legs, rather than the outside as I have always done. I was also concerned about my tendency to get my weight too far forward toward my toes, throwing my balance off, and I wanted to curb my tendency to get my left side too far in front of the ball and my right side ahead of the ball.

If you make a strong left-side move but you get somewhat outside the left leg and you don't let the arms get the free ride described in *Five Lessons*, you will find yourself chopping straight down on the ball, from ahead of it, rather than trapping the ball in the midst of the forward transition, resulting in an inability to release strongly through the ball. You just get jammed up, unable to power through impact. I hit the ball farther left at times and blocked it equally right other times, real mystery military golf (left, right, left.) If I had to play for score, I hit nothing but five-woods off the tee and knockdowns to everything but the greenest of flags (lights, that is, as in a safe flag to aim at). The minute I let a full swing fly, there was no telling what the result would be, which made for some lively discussions about windows, houses, and lawsuits in some of the crowded golf-course housing developments on the courses in Northern Virginia!

I made the Little League and Senior League All Star Team playing shortstop growing up, and later played military softball. I had great difficulty cultivating the feeling or sensation that I was making a play that I had perfected by age eleven, which was making the sidearm throw to first base. I had done it ten thousand times or more in my life, so I knew the feeling intuitively, but had not done it in fifteen years or so, nor ever felt it in my golf swing. I also did not feel like I was holding the angle well enough, either, which became an active element of my swing only when I began holding my right side, including my head, behind the ball, emphasizing the *Five Lessons* recommendation to stabilize and hit off the right side, but more specifically, the inside right side. But it has to stabilize while the left side is moving out! I also reemphasized watching the back of the ball with my dominant or left eye, as an aggressive move forward or off the ball like I did for years, placing the weight on the outside of the left leg kills any chance of watching the club go under the ball with your left eye. In fact, my old swing wrenched my head off the ball and I often failed to keep pace with my arms. These changes made a big difference. My arms started to keep pace with my body turn, enabling good eye-ball contact and fostering a good inside move after these fundamentals were ingrained. I also took the pincer fingers (index and thumb) of my right hand off the club because I did not see any chance of having my right hand in the correct position through impact. I worked hard to ingrain the feel of an exaggerated supination of the left hand, with the right hand open relative to the ball, palm canted somewhat down, and actually feeling like it is slinging slightly through and level, rather than steeply down and up. I revisited the plane, which I had never really been comfortable with as a concept. I sheepishly admit that I did not give much thought to it at all until about July 2008 and I really got serious about it in August. I don't know why it took so long and I will explain it by saying that in the spring of 2008, I had finally ingrained just about all these elements sufficient to produce a good-feeling golf swing, using the fundamentals outlined in *Five Lessons*. But it wasn't until I was trying to ferret out why I inexplicably hit a total stinker in the middle of an otherwise exceptional ball-striking session that I resolved to narrow down the guilty parties. By stinker, I mean one where you are tempted to quickly yell, "Damn, who did *that* embarrassment?" Careful scrutiny of these bad-shot moments revealed there were three egregious or recalcitrant guilty parties, the third of which was the plane. I have a bit more to say on that aspect of the investigation later.

In the end, it is probably not of much interest how long it took me to get to the answer, because I wasn't really looking for it per se but for the last two years. I was certainly not in any danger of finding it before, either, given the lack of consistency I was achieving in my golf swing. So I am struck by how long it took to integrate the elements correctly to get to the point where I was literally forced to solve the issue.

I was merely trying to get to the point where a person who considers themselves a good athlete (as well as smart and good looking) could take the fundamentals listed in *Five Lessons* and apply them in a manner that would produce consistent swings and corresponding good golf. But this was complicated by the fact that I always pronated in my backswing, a residue, I suspect, of my baseball years.

CHAPTER TWELVE

Trials and Tribulations, Too.

"Boss, I'm not saying there has been no progress (65 days into the 30 day MASINT study). I'm saying you need a nana-meter to measure it!"
Scott Webster

I was a relative hack for a long time as a golfer; not surprising in that I did not consider golf a sport. I was not looking to improve for a long time, until I made a concerted effort, eventually improving to a two index. I achieved that at the Fort Ord Golf Course complex in Monterey that includes Blackhorse and a tough course called Bayonet. Many of the touring pros who have been through qualifying school (Q school) have nightmare memories of Bayonet. The average score for Q School during my two years there hovered over seventy-six from the tips, with medalist honors rarely under par much more than two to four strokes over six rounds, if at all, with more than ninety-nine percent of the field over par. So my two index traveled well. I played with some of the pros who came through for Q School and I was struck each time by how ordinary most of them played compared to me (ordinary means boring in this case, rarely in trouble). I played with a number of very good golfers during my time there, but as good as a two index may sound to some, it was my short game that was the highlight, as I rarely hit more than ten or eleven of fourteen fairways nor more than twelve or thirteen of eighteen greens. I had considerable difficulty moving the ball left to right, which is a polite way to say I could not do it on demand.

I played golf as a kid. My dad was a good golfer who took us kids with him to play Triggs Municipal Course, in Providence, Rhode Island. I later caddied at Alpine Country Club, Cranston, RI, for several summers, a largely Italian club with a very nice old-style golf course design. It was a great golf course and caddies could play all day on Monday. My circle of friends picked it up and eventually played quite a bit. But I played other sports, and I always wanted to get into the martial arts, influenced no doubt by Bruce Lee in the television series *The Green Hornet*. I continued to play golf periodically with my friends, who all seemed to be getting into it to varying degrees, but I never pursued it as a serious sport and quit altogether after I went in the Army in 1975.

Being in the Army afforded me little time to pursue golf, anyway, although I did play other sports. I played post-level tennis, finishing second in the post-singles championship two years in a row and winning the doubles championship both years, qualifying for the Western Forces Command Championships at Presido of San Francisco and Ft. Lewis, Washington, respectively. Not much golf played during the years I was stationed overseas, but to show what an optimist I was, I played Ramstein Air Force Base Golf Course with friends, and they were selling a Hogan Apex one-iron for five dollars and I bought it. It had a sweet spot the size of the fingernail on your pinky and I am hardpressed to explain how or why I hit that club so well, but it was my only club for several years and it was perfect to tee off with, normally going pretty straight and good for 240 yards. But I played golf infrequently from 1975 to 1990. I did not own a set of clubs, just the one-iron.

One memorable round happened when I returned from Korea in 1981. I had only been home about six days and I had an itch to play golf. My wife went with me for the first and only time, and rode in the cart. On the second hole I hit a seven-iron to a 167-yard par three and the ball looked like it was right on the edge of the cup. As I was explaining how close it looked, it dropped in for a hole in one! I started yelling and my wife was a bit embarrassed, wondering what all the fuss was about. Of course I breathlessly explained to her that it was a hole-in-one, that I hit it from the tee and it went in the hole. And she replied, deadpan, "Isn't that what you are supposed to do?"

It remains the only hole-in-one I've ever had (and the only time she ever went with me.) Around 1990 or '91, I was talked into playing Army intramural golf and decided life was too short to play so badly. I decided I wanted to play more golf and become a better golfer. Up to that time, although I hit the ball well, I shot in the high eighties to low nineties, played eight or nine times in a good year, and never thought much about improving my golf. I usually played when my family visited to spend time with my father.

So I started from a terrible state at an eighteen-plus handicap, and steadily improved to a twelve, if I can say that, by studying David Ledbetter's instruction manual *The Golf Swing* and the accompanying tape developed in consultation with Nick Faldo. I had never thought about the golf swing in a critical way until I read his book.

The idea of what I was trying to accomplish with my golf swing all changed one memorable day for me, when as mediocre golfers are wont to do from time to time, I made a putt or two and was three under par on the front nine at TPC Starr Pass in Tucson, Arizona. I came to a hole with a green shaped like an hourglass or a vertical bow tie, with the pin in the center portion. I hit a great one-iron for position and hit a pretty sand wedge that took one hop, hit the flag stick halfway up, then fell off the green to the left, leaving an uphill, fluffy, smothered lie. I chopped it out and ended up making bogey. Shortly thereafter I hit a pretty three-wood layup up the right side of a left dogleg and, to my dismay, the ball took off like a kangaroo and ended up in an uphill, side hill, gnarly lie next to the cart path. The ball had hit a sprinkler head in the fairway so, instead of being in the gravy spot, I was in a very difficult situation. Also, between self-pity at my bad luck and my increasing aggravation, I was working up to a lathery, slow boil.

My next shot put me over the top, as my nine-iron went right under the ball and the ensuing flop shot went about ten yards. I was so angry at blowing my great front-nine score that I grabbed my pitching wedge and made an instinctive hard swing at the ball and just flushed it. It clanked like a shank but the ball made a ricochet sound coming off the clubface and literally "buzzed" or "fizzed" as it moved out. It was so loud that my playing partner and I thought I hit a rock, although there was no visible mark on my clubface. The ball flew some 140 yards well to the back of the green and proceeded to spin clear off the front of the green, having backed up some sixty or seventy feet. It spun so far back it made both of us laugh at the ridiculous sequence of events. My playing partner was the one prone to volcanic fits, and if he reads this he will surely remember the time at

Fort Huachuca where the more athletic of us had to climb a tree to retrieve his misbehaving nine-iron, so it was ironic that I was the one losing it. Actually, I had to climb the tree that day to avoid getting hurt, as the sight of him trying to climb the tree and having his beer belly contact trunk and reject his body three times in a row had me laughing so hard, and him so angry, that something was going to have to give! I had no idea what I had done, other than swing out of anger, but it was a fairly rare event at that time for me, a 10-12 handicapper, to get that type of spin on the ball, or much spin at all. Needless to say, I did not routinely hit my pitching wedge 140 yards. I was normally content if it went close to where I aimed and landed anywhere in the vicinity.

    I worked to replicate the swing for the remainder of the day, ruining my golf score in the process. I knew I had inadvertently stumbled on a natural feeling swing that moved me through the correct positions instinctively, whether through anger, pure luck, or whatever. But in truth, I was a terrible golfer who probably should have sought professional instruction. I did get fitted by a local club maker shortly thereafter, and he scrupulously set the clubs up through three fittings for my swing. I was somewhat disturbed to see the clubs when he completed them, as they looked open at address in a way that was not pleasing to the eye, and I had difficulty soling them at address. No matter how hard I tried to sole the club, the toe or the heel appeared to be off the ground and canted away from me. But I hit them on the screws, right in the center of the clubface. I just had trouble looking at them at address. Everyone I played with asked to see them, because they looked so unusual. When I got on the golf course hitting the ball, I usually did very well once I got my bad stretch out of my system. But I struggled to get in a comfortable position over the ball to the point where I would routinely shoot 41-43 on the front, give up the proverbial mechanical ghost, and just try to hit shots and shape the ball on the back. I invariably shot 37-39 on the back nine. I rarely put two good nines together. I always started my round focused on swing mechanics. At some point during the round I inevitably became frustrated, abandoned the focus on mechanics and did the opposite, just trying to hit shots and paying no attention to mechanics. Most of the books at the time focused on mechanics and not hitting shots, so I just thought my technique was faulty. But I puzzled over why my best scores were achieved when I focused on the shot at hand and not on the mechanics that were apparently so all-important. And I did not have much time to work on my golf game.

After the incident at Starr Pass, I spent a lot of time hitting golf balls at odd hours, often at five a.m. at the local driving range, trying to replicate the feeling of that swing. I thought if I could get my arms synchronized with my hips as they torque, I should be able to repeat my swing time after time. It may sound silly, but I wanted to ingrain the feel of that swing so I could repeat it after my next extended layoff.

My work at the time included 343 days of travel in thirty-four months. That is not a complaint, just a fact. Most people enjoyed the travel, but I had more than my share. Some of the test officers that served at the same time had been involved in two to four tests during their assignment. I took part in sixteen. It was a great experience working with some incredible people, but it did not help or facilitate my goal of improving my golf.

During this time, the better golf I played, the more chances I had for birdies and the occasional eagle, and I found that my natural putting stroke did not perform well under pressure. After choking like a dog during several rounds where I faced the prospect for shooting personal bests, I resolved to do something systematic as a way to improve my short game. I stumbled onto the Paul Runyon methodology I mentioned earlier and committed to adopting it completely while I worked on the rest of my game. Little did I know it would take almost two years to ingrain the fundamentals and get the measure of it as a natural feeling replacement for my instinctive play around the green.

Throughout much of this time, I continued the martial arts training I started in 1976 and was teaching a number of classes, including the Advance Black Belt class at Jae Kim's Tae Kwon Do in Sierra Vista, Arizona. I had also been studying other arts, such as Hap Kido and Tang Soo Doo, as well as Jeet Kune Do. Much of the analogy to my golf game I increasingly found in Bruce Lee's approach to his art, described in Jeet Kune Do. He dissected the art form, broke down each nuanced movement of the things that worked, implemented elements from other arts, including Ju Jitsu, grappling, Puerto Rican stick fighting, Kung Fu, Judo, and many others, to found Jeet Kune Do. He also mastered the one-inch punch. My work with this technique convinced me it had applications for golf and through that application I discovered what I later learned was the knockdown shot. The one-inch punch is an amazing technique and I have demonstrated an ability to move two pretty good-sized human beings several feet backwards, to the point where they are pushed off their feet.

What does Bruce Lee have to do with golf? During his journey to perfect his art, Lee focused on each of the elements, kick, punch, stance, etc., with a life-and-death seriousness. But once he gained mastery of the techniques, Bruce Lee stated that he learned in the end that a punch was just a punch, a kick was just a kick. Once he mastered the art, he no longer thought in terms of canned responses or a mechanical approach to offense or defense. He let his body instinctively use the techniques he had mastered through the learning of his art. There was only the direction of an uncluttered mind. I increasingly thought of my tendency to shoot better scores when I focused on the shot required, and not on the swing mechanics or fundamentals as an issue that was analogous to Bruce Lee's example. I also learned that a partial swing with proper fundamentals provided a good basis for keeping the ball in play and posting a score, which was important for intramurals where we only played nine holes and I often went directly from the car to the first tee. I averaged a shade over forty in the year-and-a-half or so that I played, which was an improvement of five strokes and three positions on the team over the course of that time period, and pretty good in hindsight when you consider that I never hit a practice ball before playing and I was never much lower than a twelve handicap. When our top player retired, I played the number-one spot the last six or seven matches and held my own, while being exposed to some pretty good golf.

I had just started reading different books to see what old-school golfers had to say about mechanics and I found *Five Lessons* about that time. I found Hogan's analogies about getting into a position to throw a punch from his golf stance an interesting link to my training. He also sought to eliminate doubts on the golf course by rehearsing everything on the practice tee, to the point where he never faced a shot he hadn't already worked on and the actual golf was somewhat anti-climactic. He sought to reduce the vagaries of play to an ability to produce the type of shot required under the circumstances, dictated by the moment and not by mechanics or simply hitting a ball the yardage you had practiced. He played in an era where he judged the yardage by eye and feel, and he actually eschewed the incorporation of yardage books in his play long after it had been adopted by all the pro golfers around him.

To me this was analogous to what I was already learning about my ability to shoot better when I hit shots rather than focus on mechanics and also analogous to Bruce Lee's approach to the mastery of his art. From the standpoint of applicability to my own trials and tribulations, I studied Hogan's fundamentals more and more, as I soon realized that the positions of his body, particularly the lower body, were analogous to martial arts base positions. I became convinced that I shared one objective with Hogan that must have been the premise for his swing from the get go, namely, trying to synchronize the movement of the arms with the rotation of the hips. Being positioned to throw a punch resonated with me, but the use of the inside muscles was a puzzlement at the time, mainly because I put my weight well outside my left leg.

  I was playing at Randolph Park, Tucson, and I broke my favorite seven-iron, hitting a normal shot, and then my four-iron. They just snapped off at the hosel during normal swings. It was apparent my "odd-looking" clubs were due for replacement, since, coupled with previous breaks, this left me with a rental-like set, consisting of the three, five, nine, and PW. Increasing use had finally done in my odd-looking clubs. I happened on Nevada Bob's at the right time, just as a consignment set of the fairly new Hogan Edge irons was being put on the floor. I bought them and asked the club fitter if he could set them up like mine. He thought I was joking, as he told me that my old set had been "beaten into submission." He could tell by looking at them that they were not suitable as the basis to adjust the new ones and he was surprised that I had used them that day! He recommended I play with the Edges and get them adjusted once I was used to them. Because I naturally pronated on the backswing, this relatively trivial but important incident may have set me back several years in my quest to perfect my swing, as I would not rediscover the importance of the club setup to my swing until well into 2005 or 2006. One of the more important aspects being the relatively flat lie required to accommodate my swing.

  I did not play for several months and was transferred to Monterey, California, in April 1992. This coincided with a time when I was stagnating around a 10 handicap. I stopped teaching Tae Kwon Do and committed to improving my golf. I fell in with a gang-some at Fort Ord that played skins and games, with the first five or six tee times Saturday and Sunday mornings. In my case, my technique was faulty and while I was really close to cleaning it up on a number of levels, I might as well have been learning about it through badminten lessons.

I could really spin those Edges and I could hit them solid. But the turning point for me was when I became frustrated by my inability to hit the ball left to right. I had always been a slicer, but as my handicap lowered and I got better, there came a point where I could not fade the ball without drastic measures that were not reliable. My draw became a raging hook at times, so bad that I could be a danger to people at the range (Fort Ord's range complex supporting Bayonet was an extended horseshoe or crescent shape. A duck hook puts people in play!). It seemed strange that in a matter of a year or so, I had gone from a dangerous slicer to an occasionally uncontrollable hooker of the golf ball. I heard through a friend that the library in Pacific Grove had a great selection of golf books. I went there one Saturday afternoon with my kids, taking Hogan's *Five Lessons* with me. I had increasingly returned to his book since my action felt very similar to his (at least in my mind.) One of the references in the library was the famous *Life* magazine cover and article from August 8, 1955. I was shocked and elated when I read the magazine, as many of the struggles I was encountering were detailed in that article.

Additionally, I read somewhere around this time that Hogan's clubs, with their wide open look and flattened lies, reminded people of "hockey sticks." Well, I was a hockey player and I found it interesting that the clubs that I had been fitted for in Sierra Vista that looked so displeasing to the eye, well, that's what they had reminded me of at the time! Course, I played hockey left-handed, not right, and I had not been able to put my finger on that aspect of the clubs until I read about it in the reference.

There was another gnawing problem for me in spite of my elation, which was that I had been struggling with the same type of issues, but I was already "naturally" using pronation or the twist of the wrist, and had been doing so for many years, I just didn't know what it was called. Supination was a bit confusing for me, as I did not feel it was consistently relevant or operative in my swing. So I took up my practice with renewed interest, but I was still somewhat wary that in spite of my elation at discovering some commonality with the "Great Ben Hogan," I did not see how this would lead to a solution since most of what I had already instinctively incorporated in my own swing and tried was the subject of the article. And *Five Lessons* came after the article, so it seemed like Hogan streamlined the instruction to the essential pieces, deliberately leaving out unnecessary elements, which must have, in the final analysis, included deliberate pronation.

So in the end, I could not convince myself that I had gleaned anything new. The biggest change I tried to make during this time was the adhesion of the arms and the feeling of using the inside muscles vice outside, of the arms, which was a radical difference in my approach to my swing. Nonetheless, attempting to recreate my Starr Pass swing and referring to the Hogan *Five Lesson's* and the article, I worked down to a two index over the next year.

As I mentioned earlier, a two index from the tips at Bayonet traveled well, and I shot in the seventies on all the courses of the Monterey Peninsula, as well as an eighty-something at Pebble Beach in the weeks following Tom Kite's U.S. Open victory, on what I can easily say were the worst greens on the peninsula and the worst I had ever played on for a good course (a judgment tainted by thirty-five putts, which was a bit unusual for me.) I think anyone who has played late afternoon at Pebble when the Poa Ana grass has grown "heady," carrot-toppy, and scratchy can probably relate. Have you ever been extremely nervous over a routine two- or three-foot putt? I hadn't before that round. Ever consistently spend a minute or more carefully replacing your ball on your marker because it just would not settle (in non-windy conditions)? I hadn't in such benign conditions. My best rounds during this time were: a 68 at Old Del Monte, a 70 on Bayonet, a 65 at Naval Post Grad (easy course with par 69) and a remarkable 78 on Blackhorse where I shot 46 and 32 and took five skins!

The book *The Search for the Perfect Swing* provided additional evidence that the techniques used by Hogan were correct and clarified a misperception that I suspect I share with most golfers about the clubface at contact and the arms through impact – the fact that the arms are not both straight until after impact, which is the only time in the swing where they are both straight and its only for a brief moment in time. But I never achieved the consistency I was looking for and I never felt like I had "it." I knew I had missed whatever Hogan discovered that allowed him to be so consistent and I was becoming convinced he was just good, with superior talent, and was able to get consistent through a lifetime of practice. I retired from the Army, hit balls for awhile and I had one last go at "it" in the several months that lapsed before I started my next job. I was convinced I was not that close to mastering the fundamentals, as I shot 76-82 or 84 in the 1994 Sierra Vista City Championships and pretty much gave up golf for several years.

I took a job working at my former military unit as a civilian and I was on travel 169 days my first year of work, supporting U.S. Central Command's Theater Missile Defense experiments. Golf was pretty much out of the question, but I continued my study efforts and analysis. I had become convinced that I was close to a good swing and also intrigued by the prospect of what I could have possibly missed in Hogan's instruction about the fundamentals and consistency, noting the continued controversy over the "secret," the results of *The Search for the Perfect Swing*, etc.

I started putting together the things I did and did not know about the swing, reviewing my journals documenting my improvement from 1991-94, separating facts from fiction, and isolating things I had documented through my own journals and those I had read. I worked to eliminate the non-essential, and also to isolate those that merited investigation. I was not looking for a secret; I was looking for the reason the instructions outlined in *Five Lessons* had not resulted in more consistency for my game.

I moved back east and I found time to hit balls again. I was right back to where I was before in the investigation. I was an easy six-ten handicap without much playing, and I improved considerably with just a little practice. I had a grooved swing action but lacked some key or critical understanding of technique that would put me over the top to produce a more consistent result. I played sporadically for the next ten years or so, and my study and analysis efforts convinced me that the "so-called" secret, if there was one, could not have anything to do with the swing at all. After all, Hogan himself said that everything he knew about the swing was "in there," referring to *Five Lessons*, and he had added words to the effect that the fortunate player was the one whose fundamentals were basically sound and therefore, aligned well with the provided instructions. But the former did not seem to track, as there was nothing about pronation in there from a positive standpoint, only an example to avoid, with the exception of the updated portion of the new foreword to the book.

I arrived at a point where I thought I had enough information to put together the sequence of Hogan's improvement, including his success in the late 1930s that had carried through to the period covering World War II and postwar until 1946. But he exhibited problems at times over the years from 1938-42 and started losing whatever thread he held in 1945-46 when, much like falling off the wagon, he began to have problems with the rattlesnake again. So he obviously found something different starting in 1946 and that element was the one that contributed to him declaring that he found the secret. I did not spend a lot of time thinking about the secret, but much of his instruction made sense to me in the context of *Five Lessons* and his hip-to-hip drill, which I used whenever there was a bet on the line and I needed to keep the ball in play. I could play to a four or five index with the restricted swing. But it was boring golf compared to my ten-twelve index playing military golf (left, right, left.)

I worked on a couple of fundamental issues that I felt were different in my own swing. These related to the right arm and the position of the right hand at impact, the position of the right side of the body, and the head in particular in relation to the ball at impact, the stability of the right side, and the grip. I was capable of watching the ball right through impact, although I rarely did it because I needed to watch the ball. When I focused on watching the club hit the back of the ball, I noticed a considerable difference in the crispness of my contact because of the restriction it puts on the forward movement of the body, but mainly the head. I also started to think about the use of the inside muscles of the arms a bit more and focused on the positions in Jules Alexander's exquisite photographs.

I don't know when it dawned on me to consider the problem differently, but I accrued a considerable amount of literature in the 2004-07 timeframe, including good video of Hogan at the Masters in 1967. There was a comment in one of the references from someone who said that Ben Hogan actually hit quite a lot of balls from right to left, but he had that golfer's blindness that allows one to loathe a hook and to see a fade where others are seeing a pull block or pulled fade, e.g., a draw that leaks right. I really enjoyed hitting golf balls and I still had little time for the five- or six-hour rounds entailed in playing on the usual weekend. But my son started to play high school golf and we practiced or played together at Virginia Oaks or Fort Belvoir, and I helped him with his swing to a degree. Later, he was working at Stonewall Golf Club in Haymarket and we often played when there was a break in the action.

At some point I decided I was going to figure this thing out, to find a way to get more consistent, if I had to reduce my swing to nothing but knockdowns, e.g., nine o'clock on the backswing and relatively no follow-through. With the new soft and thin-covered golf balls, there was no issue with a lack of backspin that plagued earlier efforts to gain consistency through a shorter swing (by limiting spin and adversely affecting control.) The breakthrough for me was the admonition to use the inside muscles of the arms, rather than the outside muscles, and the plane. What's the difference, you wonder? Picture the motion of compressing an accordion closed and then pulling it open with both arms in a motion that keeps the upper arms tight (with biceps pressed against the upper body) and uses mostly the forearms and hands. Ever feel that kind of motion in a golf swing? How about starting a lawn mower, pulling the chord toward your shoulder with your foot braced on the engine? How about opening the refrigerator or freezer door? Not the initial pull, but the actual opening part? If there is a visual to think about, it might be a hammer thrower, with the position of the hips and the arms, with the hammer coming through for the last turn, thinking about the speed or running start the hips and pivoting body give the arms. The hammer is being pulled by inside pull or force. I also thought about the one-inch punch example and the push or thrust off the right side.

Finally, the matter of the plane. I knew my position was perfect when I hit a draw, e.g., my left leg brace, my hip turn, my right arm movement, the tension between upper and lower body, the feeling of supination through the ball, the feeling of slinging or trapping vice hitting the ball, with the body almost directly over the ball and trapping it, the pure feeling of contact, etc. The feeling reminds me of squeezing a grape out of its skin, the sense of literally extruding the ball out of the middle of your dynamic movement forward in the midst of the swing motion. The left side moves aggressively and the right side thrusts out of the backswing to keep pace, but the body is somewhat behind the ball at contact. The thrust is distinctive and visible in most videos of Hogan, evidenced by the slide or movement of his right foot forward to keep his balance point centered, with almost all the weight leftward. That was the feeling of the swing at Starr Pass described earlier, and I could repeat it when I hit a draw. But I was not consistent with the results, even though I felt I was repeating it time after time.

I discovered over time that even though I was trying to swing the same way each time, when I hit a fade I unconsciously changed my action to the point where it was not the same swing at all. My swing thought for my attempts at fading the ball was my version of Freddy Couple's swing, upright, outside, free flow, and full. My weight tended toward my toes and I had balance issues. I could feel the positions were markedly different and I was getting erratic and inconsistent shots. At some point in my review of the fundamentals all of a sudden it struck me that something I had never paid much attention to was the plane and its relationship to my shots. The Couple's swing image was great for a fade thought, but I needed to replace the relatively upright plane after each use!

I started to notice in my practice sessions that a big problem was my lack of consistency on the position of the club on the backswing, as I was getting upright and toe bound when I was consciously hitting a fade. I isolated the movement through abbreviated swings or knockdowns of increased swing length over the course of a number of practice sessions and I started to pay attention to the path by concentrating more deliberately on the waggle to guide the backswing path. I categorically and definitively, through a control approach of repeating swings, narrowed down my problem to an inability to get through the ball or the feeling that I was jamming up at release. I at times had the feeling of coming somewhat over the top, with causality attributable to coming into the ball from too steep a swing-path angle, resulting in an action whereby the right arm was swinging predominantly down and straightening on more of a vertical orientation, rather than predominantly through and inclined horizontally, like my draw swing. The hands were not working together, or properly, so when they hit the bottom of the swing arc, they stopped or more appropriately, "jammed up," rather than transitioning through, transferring momentum through the ball.

The other problem was arm speed; I was not keeping up with my body when I made partial swings or fade swings. I was unconsciously slowing my swing, rather than maintaining my tempo. So there were a number of things to work on, and I was seemingly unable to do anything about it. The bad habits were so ingrained and for several practice sessions in a row, I was absolutely exasperated by my inability to isolate, repeat, and untangle the positions. I could not consistently go from a fade to a draw, e.g., with and without deliberate pronation, which was my natural swing (as previously mentioned) without unconsciously changing my swing. The change engendered a ruinous movement toward being upright with the swing plane that would dash any hope of hitting good shots. At the very least, I could not alter from one to the other (draw to fade) and was inconsistent in execution between the long and short irons. The good news was that I stumbled onto a portion of the puzzle that eluded me before, which was the true importance of the plane. But that was still about the opposite position espoused by most of the swing gurus, who advocated either a more upright plane or a plane that did not vary from backswing to follow through. And I was continually struggling to keep my weight centered or back toward my heels. So what to do?

I revisited the fundamentals as I knew them and spent some time working through them on the range. I started to adopt a warm-up drill that I had first heard attributed to Hogan, involving setting up with everything square to the target line, with very little body movement, to concentrate on pulling the arms through while de-emphasizing the hands and with a nine o'clock or left arm parallel swing with a pitching wedge. I really started to focus on my grip, waggle, and the delivery position. Several practice sessions in a row I spent almost half the time and half the balls moving through the bag focusing on this technique, which was a bland knockdown shot that went mainly straight and rarely hooked.

When I added my normal wrist cock, two faults appeared immediately; the primary one was coming over the top by getting too steep with my backswing plane, which caused the hitting action to get outside the main line (hit from the outside path rather than the inside path), while also moving my weight too much forward to my toes, which caused balance issues. The other problem was too much emphasis on the hands. It was only too handsy or too over-the-top if I had my weight too much on my toes or if I lifted the club up rather than swinging it around. I put even more emphasis on the waggle as a way to set the path of the backswing to help prevent or eliminate a tendency to get upright. The more I stayed back, the better I hit the ball, and the more I moved my alignment point left of the target to help the hips open and free the body to release the arms. The more I rolled the clubface open and hit the slot on the backswing, the more I found that I had to aim right of the target, as I had started pulling the ball left in what was not a hook or draw, but a pull that faded or drifted right at the end. I had several sessions where I hit the wooden posts marking the distances with consecutive shots, hitting four in a row one day. And I mean the six-inch post, not the sign.

I was still having some difficulty hitting a deliberate fade or slice, as my swing would get steep the minute I tried to consciously get much left to right movement. The steep plane simply impedes supination by causing the hands to jam together at the bottom of the swing arc. I increasingly focused on rolling the clubface open and thinking more in terms of a draw or hook action, since

I had become convinced from watching recent releases of Hogan that he was hitting with a deliberate draw or hook swing, regardless of what he or anyone else believed or had publicly said. The more I trained myself to back off on the hands, the more I pulled the ball, but the less I drew it. I stopped hooking with this technique unless I did something radically wrong. The ball just exploded off the club toward the twelve o'clock position and stayed mainly straight. I figured out that the fade or slice swing thought had been ingrained in my swing as a lifting of the arms, which forced a coming over the top move that prevented proper natural release of the hands via supination. By getting steep with the swing, the hands were approaching the ball at an angle of attack that restricted supination without some type of further manipulation.

    I worked on developing an image of my swing that would help eliminate the bad swing when I transitioned from a draw to a fade action. I thought about swinging a long hose or rope, which was quite a bit behind the body and needed to be swung very low and deliberately forward so as not to kink it or prevent its cracking like a whip as it went forward. The steeper it was swung or yanked, the less likely it would produce a controlled crack. For those who have chopped wood or swung an axe, a fairly level swing is the most effortless way to go to prevent exhausting yourself. Can you properly swing and chop with an axe without adopting a decent golf power transition position? Watch some video of the lumberjack competitions in action to see what I mean.

    So the combination of a steep plane and poor posture or improper weight distribution had caused me to lift the hands higher, even while I was rolling the clubface open, which emphasizes the hands. That was the opposite of what I was trying to do. I had learned a flop shot modeled after Freddy Couple's swing that went immediately upright and outside to inside, which was increasingly the cause of the ruinous motion. I hit the shot great, but it was ruinous for the next shot, where the mental imagery of that shot was being processed for application to the next one. I also experimented with flattening the lofts of my clubs and thickened my grips throughout this period of experimentation, verifying that my natural swing requires more flattened lies.

    At some point after several sessions working through the mechanics (and I should add that I had learned to focus on mechanics on the range, intermixed with shots, and hitting nothing but shots with no mechanics other than a knockdown thought on the golf course) I became frustrated at my inability to separate the swing objectives and execute the proper movements. I gave it considerable thought and reviewed the aspects that I had worked on for several months. I realized the problem was somewhat artificial, because my drill to isolate the hands was not a fade or a draw swing, per se. It was just a swing to isolate the hands by eliminating them.

But I had been thinking about mechanics for so long that I instinctively thought in terms of the result and it was clear that this influenced my swing. So I hit on the idea of not thinking about hitting a fade or a draw at all, but focusing on swinging as if I was making a proper swing to isolate the hands, regardless of my actual intent, and to work, through either alignment or grip, or sometimes both, to compensate to achieve the desired effect, e.g., a shot that drew or faded. That way I could make the same swing each time with my normal action and compensate through alignment and body positions or the position of my hands on the club, rather than actively changing anything about the swing itself. In actuality, I would make my natural draw action each time, but I could not risk thinking about it that way. Thinking about hitting a fade using a draw action gets just plain complicated! But the point is that since I knew my action and the position of my body was perfect (feel-wise) when I hit a draw, then the idea was to hit a draw every time, even when I was trying to hit a fade.

The culmination of these efforts was several practice sessions where I hit the ball dead solid and as well as I can hit it when I dropped the pronation and just made a swing that produced a draw. But I continued to have difficulty with my normal pronation swing and my attempts to fade the ball. One day at the range I hit several perfect draws in a row with the swing that felt a bit awkward for me (no pronation) followed by several bad normal swings where I attempted to hit it straight or fade it. I was hitting the ball as well and in fact better than ever before by September 2008. I was beginning to think I was just not capable of getting "it." I hit a perfect draw with my best club, the seven-iron, which is the club I learned with growing up, hitting the 160-yard sign from about 168 yards out dead center with a draw shot, only to hit the very next attempt with my normal swing dead left. I shrugged it off and hit another draw, just missing the post of the 160 marker to the left by less than a foot. I made another attempt with my normal swing and pushed it right to where I missed the green. I hit another draw shot that went directly over the 160 sign, only to hit another shot wide left with my normal swing.

I cleaned my club, put the club down and went into the driving range shop to get a soda. I wracked my brain to work through what would cause such a disparity between the results when I was clearly hitting the ball as well as I was capable of hitting a golf ball. I gave some thought to just dropping my normal swing action in favor of just hitting a draw all the time, but one of the problems was the draw becoming a raging hook at times. It then dawned on me that the only difference between the two shots was my thought process of trying to hit a fade vice a draw, and my normal pronation move in the backswing. So I decided to make the same exact swing intending a different result, e.g., a draw on the one hand and a fade on the other with the same swing, that is my draw-swing thought. While that may not sound like a big difference, when I returned to the tee my draw shot just missed the sign to the left, and my fade shot hit the sign dead center! I was shocked given the recent previous sequence of events and given the results of my last several practice sessions. I went through several sequences of draws and fades and repeated it thereafter, although not hitting the sign immediately. But it worked so well when I tried it that this was one of the first times I ever took the time to get a second bucket at the range. I hit every yardage pole up to the 275-yard marker that day moving through the bag. A bucket has one hundred-twenty balls in it, so this is serious ball bashing. The second bucket I hit mostly four-irons, alternating between a draw and a fade, with the only difference being the addition or dropping of the pronation or cup of the wrist. I accomplished something that day that I had never been able to do, which is to hit high and low draws and fades, as well as straight balls, knockdown shots and crazy slices, high and low fades, etc. I hit them one after the other with little to no transition time, without hitting bad shots or having the problems I previously described.

I was somewhat hesitant to stop hitting balls that afternoon, as I had a nagging fear that, much like lightning in a bottle, some confluence of swing "luck" had coalesced for me that afternoon, never to be repeated again. I could not wait to get back the next day, as I had hit almost two hundred-forty balls or so and did not hit ten bad shots in the last one hundred-forty-five. I had been on good streaks at the range before, but nothing close to that kind of consistency. Hitting twenty-five or thirty bad ones out of one hundred-twenty was more typical for me, as I usually started dropping off noticeably from the five- to the three-iron. The next day I hit about seventy balls before I missed a shot and it was a shock when it happened! Out of one hundred-twenty balls, I hit most great with about five bad shots. (I have to either relearn the flop shot or just be real careful with my "Freddy Couple's move!")

CHAPTER THIRTEEN

What Do You Do Once You Know?

"The future is so bright you have to wear sunglasses."
Ted Cope

The last part of my story unfolded over the past two years, as I was still somewhat busy running a large government program, and I was a bit distracted by that matter. I was not working it full-time, obviously, and I was still somewhat plodding along, eliminating or isolating one fault at a time as I worked the kinks out of my swing. I spent my time after the "breakthrough" in September of 2008 until November of that year trying to convince myself that I still had work to do on my swing. I reread every Hogan reference I had and sought those that I lacked in my library. In December I became convinced that I had followed the same path that Hogan had in ferreting out his secret in 1946, and also became convinced that this is what Henny Bogan did for Ben Hogan so many years ago.

As I have said, Henny Bogan was the opposite of Ben Hogan. He could not hook the ball and he had a very weak grip. He cupped his wrist, swung relatively flat and his swing went in an exaggerated manner around his body. Good golfers struggle with a hook and Henny was desperate to draw the ball, but the combination of his weak grip, flat lies, weakened lofts, and open clubfaces precluded him from hooking no matter how hard he tried. The only way he could hook was to drop the cup in his wrist; that is, to swing like Ben Hogan. The funny thing that happened to Ben Hogan is that while Henny Bogan was attempting to prove that he was not a hack after all and that he could hook the ball, he taught Ben Hogan that his swing was ideal to produce a fade, as long as he worked very hard to draw the ball, that is, to take his normal swing. As long as all things were equal, that is. He had oversized grips that made it difficult to use his hands, he had stiff shafts so he knew exactly where the head of the club was at release, he flattened his lies, weakened his lofts to open his clubface and stayed on a relatively flat plane and most of all, he kept his hands pretty much out of the swing, resulting in the delayed hit and hinged lever action that was the envy of *The Search for the Perfect Swing* study.

When I discovered that this worked best with my normal action, that is, a swing that should ordinarily produce a hook, I was shocked! I worked hard to prove myself wrong in this regard, as it seemed just preposterous, but when I utterly convinced and deluded myself that I was trying to hit a hook every time, no matter how obvious it was that the situation called for a fade, the results were always good. Again, the draw action is perfect, providing you have the elements of the swing as outlined in *Five Lessons,* e.g., sound basic fundamentals.

With hands on top of the grip, my lies a bit flat and my clubface slightly open, I try to hit a draw each time and I generally produce a pull that fades slightly or goes straight. A key for me is to move aggressively to the left side but to keep the head in place and my dominant or left eye on the back of the ball. I see the club hit the ball when I hit a good shot. Most of my bad shots are a result of my head moving forward to the point where I can't see the back of the ball. But I also had several lapses during my sessions where I forget to attempt to draw, or I put a slice swing on it by coming over the top unconsciously, or I leaned forward on my toes and wrecked the synchronization of the arms and body, getting stuck at the bottom because of a faulty weight transfer. It ruins the whole affair. The right arm straightens prematurely, or comes away from the hip. The clubface sweeps to the left through the ball like it is supposed to, but not from the inside; it sweeps from the outside.

David Leadbetter captured this well in his book *The Fundamentals of Hogan*, although his explanation on how Hogan did this is incomplete. You cannot be above plane and sweep through properly as depicted in his book on page 115, e.g., inside to inside "fast left." Ironically, I also started to hit the ball farther and straighter, with even more spin, which is important when you throttle back to hit knockdown shots. But it is extremely difficult to do this consistently within a normal pre-shot routine. You must somehow delude yourself into thinking one way while hitting the other.

I worked on my aim and alignment for the middle to short irons and found that my aim point needed to be somewhat right or toward the one o'clock position, with the target at twelve o'clock and my body aligned to eleven o'clock or so. That is a stark contrast to the club being aligned directly to the target and everything parallel left, which is detailed in *Five Lessons*. In aligning, I am focusing on pulling or slinging the ball across the target and then drifting it back slightly. It is a feeling similar to hitting a sliding sidespin forehand or backhand in tennis that moves away from you as it takes the spin, but with an actual technique the opposite to achieve the result, much like an American Twist serve (you are slicing or brushing aggressively across the ball from about eight o'clock to two o'clock,) where the ball is going to bound the opposite way as appears. In doing this I simplified my action significantly and discovered why my problems of the past really stemmed from a faulty swing plane, rather than a faulty swing or bad positions. An oversimplified example is a bunt in baseball. Really talented hitters can stab at the ball with the bat oriented on an angle, but parallel to the ground and extended across the plate increases the odds of hitting the ball for the average hitter. You can cast a rod and reel from the side and hit targets straight in front of you, but if the target is straight in front of you, why complicate things by casting sidearm – just cast straight.

I examined the problem with a different approach and discovered to my delight, that it worked. I looked upon Hogan with new respect. Can you imagine the type of discipline it takes to aim slightly right of a mid-left target and pull it left, having faith that it will fade back to the right as long as you commit to the shot as if you are hitting a hook? And having been a hooker all your life, not backing off or flinching with the fear that the ball might actually hook? Think about the pressure-packed tee shot he hit four days in a row to hole number six, Carnoustie, in the 1953 Open. A hook or draw of any sort is usually out of bounds. Wow.

Most of the time when hitting balls, I find that I revert back to a fade swing unconsciously, that is from outside to inside, which is the natural tendency.

I hit several balls before I realize that I've done it. The difficulty comes with hitting or manufacturing shots on the practice range and it definitely must be practiced. Ironically enough, it is much easier to do it on the golf course when there is a shot or challenge to solve than it is hitting practice balls, unless you spend huge amounts of time on the range to perfect it (hint, hint).

Did Henny Bogan play golf cursed with a slice or fade, having never learned to hook from Ben Hogan, or did Ben Hogan learn to fade or slice from Henny Bogan while never again having to suffer the curse of the hook? Or did Ben and Henny share the stage together, hitting the shots called upon during a round to produce the desired effect?

This is the type of thought process that I believe takes the story to a level where it need not go, while amplifying the reasons I provided earlier on why Hogan did not discuss this matter during his lifetime. I believe that Henny Bogan was initially employed as a lark, a semi-humorous, although desperately serious alternative approach that allowed for experiments on the range as an anti-Ben Hogan, and then kept as a reminder of the caricature of what Hogan desired to become, which is a golfer who does not struggle with a hook. That Henny Bogan is a significant part of the secret is hard to deny; he makes other appearances throughout the Hogan story, most notably for the Hogan sales staff as the guy who does not meet comportment standards and is therefore a derelict salesman nobody wants to buy from. At odd times Hogan reportedly introduced himself or even signed himself as Henny Bogan, adding credence to the theory that he really wanted to come clean with the story. But a good golfer always struggles with a hook, so again the joke is that Henny Bogan was a hacker, as he could not hook the ball, and therefore not worthy of Hogan's respect. But he really wasn't, as he actually taught the great Ben Hogan how to hit a fade and, therefore, to get good!

In the final analysis, Henny Bogan was Ben Hogan's secret weapon employed to help him scientifically isolate the movements required to master his swing and fix his hook problem. The methodology employed via Henny's effort to learn to hook helped Hogan learn to fade the ball by using his normal swing and pronation. Henny would not be much good for anyone who did not have the same action and therefore suffered from the same swing problems as Hogan. When Jack Nicklaus stated that he assumes a weakened grip and then tries as hard as he can to hook the ball, he Henny Bogan'd it as well!

So this is two of the secrets that I alluded to in the beginning of this book. One involved the mysterious Mr. Henny Bogan and what role, if any, he played in the development of the Hogan swing. As you can see, it was significant. Also, you can understand why Hogan would not have had respect for a golfer who could not hook the ball, when everyone knows a good golfer constantly fights a hook. Hogan's reticence to describe how he came by his secret is understandable. Besides not wanting to be harassed every waking hour about his secret, he certainly would not have had much patience for discussions about the practice construct that aided his investigation. Whether done as a lark, adopted like someone does when they are competing against themselves in any sport, or done because he had such powers of concentration that he could credibly replicate the opposite persona (e.g., the swing), the time for Hogan to reveal this secret bypassed him with the publishing of the *Life* magazine article.

Who knows when he first employed Henny Bogan as a learning device? Could it have been as early as the Glen Garden playoff with Bryon Nelson? The earliest reference found at this point based on my research is about 1936, which opens the possibility that Henny was involved in Hogan's successful implementation of Henry Picard's tip in 1938. One should not underestimate the difficulty golfers have in general, but Hogan in particular in the late 1930s, making swing changes during the golf season while they are playing for their livelihoods. I never had that problem or impediment, but desperation is the mother of invention, as they say.

The other subtle part of this, which I count as the second secret, is that Hogan solved his hook problem by always hitting hooks. Some with whom I have discussed this notion have rejected it out of hand, saying that from his words and watching him play, this can't possibly be correct. Hooks nauseated the man and he often played a fade even when faced with an obvious hooking opportunity. That is true and has been attributed to him, but I think closer scrutiny of how he figured his swing out and more importantly, how he deployed it, reveals consistent references to his often hitting the ball right to left, or employing his swing to pull the ball left with a fade to the correct position.

Tom Kite has been quoted as saying that Hogan aimed slightly right, while aligned slightly left and then hit it slightly off the toe, but the ball seemed to go mostly straight. Most of these shots that were pulled or slung left were not hooks or draws at all, but fades to a left position by bringing the ball in from the right, an equivalent difficulty to a draw to a right position. Obviously, at least in the latter case, a shot Hogan felt no self-respecting golfer should play. Hogan plays these shots like "slings," anyway, so it is doubtful that he even considered them pulls.

I defy anybody to look through the available pictures or swing sequences of Hogan and point out the ones in which his swing looks like he is in the process of hitting a fade (after spring 1946)! I have none in my possession! As I related earlier, when I watched the *Shell's Wonderful World of Golf* tape, I was astounded to watch him swing and then see the ball move from left to right. There are several shots where he slings it in low from left to right with a lot of spin and there is no distinguishing those swings from the others. On other holes he pulls or slings it in from right to left on a very flat trajectory with tremendous spin. The subtleties between his fade and draw swing are near miniscule in the extreme; to point this out in pictures based on Jules Alexander's photographs is difficult to do, even aided by the observations provided by Ken Venturi.

The answer is found in the follow-through and the presence of the cupped wrist. But the overall action looks exactly the same, so it can be borderline laughable to listen to or read analysis of Hogan's swing where there is no preamble that explains what Hogan was trying to accomplish with the shot, which is really the essential part of trying to figure out that particular swing. In fact, there is abundant evidence of Hogan swinging where people talk about the cup in his wrist when there is no cup there at all!

So there you have it! Henny Bogan has made an appearance and it is a significant one. Hogan solves his hook problem once and for all and never looks back. The results he produces from 1946 through 1949 and then from 1950 through 1955 or so are astounding, with 1953 perhaps the greatest year any golfer ever had, period!

The last item you might be wondering is: if I am so smart and have figured it out, what has this meant for my golf game? I had this very conversation with my wife recently. It starts: You know, this begs the question of what difference has it made in your golf game (smarty guy)? The truth is, I just figured this out for sure in late August or early September 2008. As mentioned, I spent several months trying to disprove what I had discovered. I only played one full round of golf after I figured it out; I did equal measures of spectacular and pathetic, but I still did not have the whole story worked through. I was still struggling to solidify the plane and the position of the right hand. I have the added problem: if I have anything else I have to do, I don't play golf. I can't. I've tried it before and I left the course because I couldn't concentrate. Frankly, golf is a game that is subordinate to a number of other things in my life.

Having said that, I started getting into shape for the 2009 golf season and verified through practice that I have the technique right. I also know that mastering what I want to accomplish with my swing does not mean I can reproduce it upon demand. But the gauntlet has been thrown down with this book and I think the only valid proof that the secret is solved and that it is applicable to a swing that is similar to that which required the move in the first place, e.g., a swing that produces a very natural draw because of the emphasis on the linkage of the arms with the hips, like Hogan's, is to apply it in a way that results in significant improved performance.

So, I have a goal to become a scratch golfer! I have never been better than a two index and I am a bit older now (okay, more than a bit,) so I would consider that proof positive that the riddle has been solved, at least insofar as my own trials and tribulations are concerned, including wrestling with the issue of mastering the fundamental elements of *Five Lessons*. I may just post my scores on my website as I progress and we can all judge for ourselves whether there is something here or not. I'm betting there is and I expect to have results to show for it!

BIBLIOGRAPHY & RESOURCES

Andrisani, John. *The Hogan Way*. New York, NY: Harper Collins, 2000.

Barkow, Al. *Golf's Golden Grind: The History of the Tour*. New York, NY: Harcourt Brace Jovanovich, 1974.

Barr, Jr., Art. *Ben Hogan and Buster*. PAWS, 2002.

Ballard, Jimmy, with Brennan Quinn. *How to Perfect Your Golf Swing*.

Trumbull, CT: ProGolf Digest, Inc., 1981.

Bertrand, Tom, with Printer Bowler. *The Secret of Hogan's Swing*. Hoboken, NJ: John Wiley & Sons, Inc. 2006.

Burke, Jackie Jr. *It's Only a Game*. New York, NY: Penguin Group, Inc. 2006.

Cochran, Alastair & Stobbs, John. *Search for the Perfect Swing, The Proven Scientific Approach to Fundamentally Improving Your Game*. Chicago, IL: Triumph Books, 1986, 1989, 1994, 1996.

Darracott, Clem. *Ben Hogan; In Pursuit of Perfection*. Grass Valley, CA: VHS, the Booklegger, 1967.

Davis, Martin. *The Hogan Mystique: Classic Photographs of the Great Ben Hogan*. Photographs by Jules Alexander; Essays by Dave Anderson, Ben Crenshaw, and Dan Jenkins; Commentary by Ken Venturi. Greenwich, CT: American Golfer, Inc., 2002.

DeMile, James W. *Bruce Lee's 1 and 3 Inch Power Punch*. Sedro Woolly, WA: Tao of Wind Chun Do Publications, 1975.

Dodson, James. *Ben Hogan; An American Life*. New York, NY: Doubleday, 2004.

Frost, Mark. *The Match*. New York, NY: Hyperion Books, 2007.

Harmon, Claude "Butch" Jr., with Steve Eubanks. *The Pro*. New York, NY: Crown Publishers, 2006.

Hogan, Ben. *Five Lessons; The Modern Fundamentals of Golf*. New York, NY: A.S. Barnes and Co., 1957.

_____. *Power Golf*. New York, NY: A.S. Barnes and Co., 1948.

_____. "This is My Secret." *Life*, New York, NY: Time, Inc., August 8, 1955.

Graubart, Julian I. *Golf's Greatest Championship; The 1960 U.S. Open*. New York, NY: Penguin Books, 1997.

Gregston, Gene. *Hogan The Man Who Played for Glory*. Grass Valley, CA: The Booklegger, 1996.

Leadbetter, David. *The Fundamentals of Hogan*. Chelsea, MI and New York, NY: Sleeping Bear Press and Doubleday, 2000.

_____, with John Huggan. *The Golf Swing*. New York, NY: The Stephen Greene Press, 1990.

Lee, Bruce. *Tao of Jeet Kune Do*. Burbank, CA: Ohara Publications, Inc., 1975.

McLean, Jim. *Ben Hogan The Golf Swing*. The Golf Channel Home, VHS, 2004. _____. The Ben Hogan Collection. McLean's Champions, LLC, DVD, 2006.

Palmer, Arnold, with James Dodson. *A Golfer's Life*. New York, NY: Ballantine Books, 1999.

Roosevelt, Theodore, 26th President. *Citizenship in a Republic:* "The Man in the Arena." Speech at The Sorbonne, Paris, France, April 23, 1910.

Runyan, Paul, with Dick Aultman. *The Short Way to Lower Scoring*. Norwalk, CT.: Golf Digest, Inc., 1979.

Sampson, Curt. *The Eternal Summer: Palmer, Nicklaus, and Hogan in 1960, Golf's Golden Year*. Dallas, TX: Taylor Publishing, 1992.

_____. *Hogan*. Nashville, TN: Rutledge Hill Press, 1996.

Schlee, John, with Swing Meyer. *Maximum Golf*. Columbia, SC: Acorn Sports, Inc., 1986.

Shell's Wonderful World of Golf:Hogan Vs. Snead [VHS], PGA Tour Productions, June 15, 1998.

Towle, Mike. *I Remember Ben Hogan*. Nashville, TN: Cumberland House, 2000.
Vasquez, Jody. *Afternoons with Mr. Hogan*. New York, NY: Penguin Group, 2004.

Wade, Don. *Swing Thoughts*. Chicago, IL: Contemporary Books, Inc., 1993.

Watson, Tom with Nick Seitz. *Tom Watson's Strategic Golf*. Trumbull, CT: NYT Special Services, Inc., 1993.

_____. *Tom Watson's Getting Back to Basics*. Trumbull, CT: Golf Digest/Tennis Inc., 1992.

Wimbrow, Dale. "The Guy in the Glass." *American Magazine*, Vol. CXVII, The Crowell Publishing Company, 1934.

Stoddard, Hud, "Ben Hogan's Secret." *Life,* New York, NY: Time, Inc., April 5, 1954.

ABOUT THE AUTHOR

Mark J. Choiniere was born in Orange, California, and grew up in Cranston, Rhode Island. He is a retired military officer and currently serves as a senior executive at the National Geospatial-Intelligence Agency, Bethesda, Maryland. He has been playing golf around the world for forty years. He is married with three children and three grandchildren.

Contact Mark:
mark@thesecretofhennybogan.com
http://ezinearticles.com/?expert_bio=Mark_Choiniere

Website address:
www.thesecretofhennybogan.com